The Advocacy Manual for Sexuality Education, Health, and Justice
Resources for Communities of Faith

Edited by Rev. Sarah Gibb Millspaugh

Unitarian Universalist Association

United Church Board for Homeland Ministries

BOSTON

The Sexuality Education Task Force Core Committee (1994-2000) is responsible for the development of *The Advocacy Manual for Sexuality Education, Health, and Justice* and the *Our Whole Lives* sexuality education curricula and companion resources. Members have included:

Reverend Makanah Elizabeth Morriss (UUA), co-chair
Reverend Gordon J. Svoboda II (UCC), co-chair
Reverend Cynthia Breen (UUA), co-chair
Reverend Jory Agate (UUA)
Kathleen Carlin (UCC)
Dr. Duane Dowell (UUA)
Judith A. Frediani (UUA)
Reverend Sarah Gibb Millspaugh (UUA/UCC)
Jennifer Devine (UUA)
Reverend Patricia Hoertdoerfer (UUA)
Faith Adams Johnson (UCC)

ISBN 978-1-55896-382-5

Printed in the United States of America.

10 9 8 7 6 5 4 3
14 13 12

The United Church Board of Homeland Ministries has disincorporated since this book was published. For matters related to that publisher, please contact the *Our Whole Lives* consultant at the United Church of Christ, 700 Prospect Avenue, Cleveland, Ohio, 216/736-3718.

Text Designer *Sandra Rigney*
Cover Designer *Isaac Stone*

Godfrey

Acknowledgments

This manual would not have been possible without the inspiration and guidance of many people. I am particularly thankful for the leadership of the Sexuality Education Task Force of the Unitarian Universalist Association and the United Church Board for Homeland Ministries in envisioning this manual and supporting its development at every step of the way. I wish to hold up the individual contributions of Task Force members: the Reverend Jory Agate, the Reverend Cynthia Breen, Dr. Duane Dowell, Judith A. Frediani, Jennifer Harrison, the Reverend Patricia Hoertdoerfer, Faith Adams Johnson, the Reverend Makanah Elizabeth Morriss, and the Reverend Gordon J. Svoboda II. Their guidance and feedback during this project have been invaluable.

I am grateful for the faith-based advocacy work of the Reverend J. Bennett Guess, Karl Puechl, Liz Jones, Duwayne Keller, Anne Marie Donohue, and Maggi Ruth P. Boyer, who shared their stories in this book's case studies. Thank you to the Reverend Barbara Gerlach and the Reverend Arthur S. Vaeni for preaching sermons on sexuality that had the power to inspire not only their congregations, but the faith-based sexuality education movement as a whole. Thank you to Sandy Sorensen of the United Church of Christ Office for Church and Society and the Reverend Meg Riley of the Unitarian Universalist Association Washington Office for Faith in Action for contributing insightful articles. Debra W. Haffner, the Reverend Dr. Roberta Nelson, the Reverend Joe Leonard, and the Reverend Meg Riley reviewed this manual during development and provided valuable insight. I am also grateful for the support and encouragement of the individuals on the National Council of Churches of Christ Committee on Family Ministry and Human Sexuality.

Thank you to Patricia Frevert, Joni McDonald, and Mary Benard of the Unitarian Universalist Association Office of Publications for their initiative and assistance in the development and production of this manual. Many thanks to my editor, Susan Worst, for her insight, energy, and hard work.

The Ford Foundation made this manual possible with its generous support of its development and production.

Thanks to Advocates for Youth for permission to reprint "The Role of Coalition Building in Community Education and Advocacy," "Education and Media Campaigns," and "Lobbying: The Art of Persuasion" from *Advocating for Adolescent Reproductive and Sexual Health: The Advocacy Kit*, copyright © 1996 by Advocates for Youth, 1025 Vermont Avenue, NW, Suite 200, Washington, DC 20005.

Thanks to the Public Conversations Project for permission to reprint "Distinguishing Debate from Dialogue," copyright © 1992 by Public Conversations Project, 46 Kondazian Street, Watertown, Massachusetts 02472.

Thanks to the SPIN Project for permission to reprint "Pitching Reporters."

Thanks to SIECUS for permission to reprint "Sexuality Education and the Schools: Issues and Answers," "Philosophy: Comprehensive vs. Fear-Based Sexuality Education Programs," and "Working with School Boards to Ensure Comprehensive Sexuality Education" from *The SIECUS Community Action Kit: Information to Support Comprehensive Sexuality Education*, copyright © 1997 by the Sexuality Information and Education Council of the United States, 130 West 42nd Street, Suite 350, New York, New York 10036-7802.

More thanks to SIECUS for permission to reprint "The Really Good News: What the Bible Says about Sex" by Debra W. Haffner and "Case Study: First United Methodist Church of Germantown" (originally published as "The Journey of Sexuality Educators to Faith Communities") by Maggi Ruth P. Boyer and Ann Marie Donohue from *SIECUS Report*, Vol. 26, No. 1, October/November 1997, copyright © 1997 by the Sexuality Information and Education Council of the United States, 130 West 42nd Street, Suite 350, New York, New York 10036-7802.

Thanks to the Reverend Barbara Gerlach for permission to reprint "Fidelity and Integrity: A Matter of Trust and Truth"; the Reverend Arthur S. Vaeni for permission to reprint "Sex, Life, and Liberalism"; Susan Worst for permission to reprint "Readings on Sexuality and Spirituality"; Sandy Sorensen for permission to reprint "Navigating the Political Landscape: A Roadmap for People of Faith," Rabbi Lynne Landsberg for permission to reprint "Using Religious Voices to Confront the Religious Right," and the Reverend J. Bennett Guess for permission to reprint "Case Study: Zion United Church of Christ, Henderson, Kentucky."

Rev. Sarah Gibb Millspaugh

Contents

Preface

This book is a manual for advocates of comprehensive sexuality education—education that enables young people and their families to obtain accurate information, articulate their values, develop relationship skills, and exercise responsibility in sexual relationships. *The Advocacy Manual for Sexuality Education, Health, and Justice* is a copublication of the Unitarian Universalist Association and the United Church Board for Homeland Ministries of the United Church of Christ, two religious groups that understand sexuality education as an important contribution people of faith can make to a just and healthy society.

It is our religious heritages that compel and guide us to create a safe environment within which people can come to understand and respond to the challenges facing them as sexual beings. We are grounded as faith communities in a common and continuing promotion of justice for all people. We affirm the dignity of the individual, the importance of personal responsibility, and the essential interdependence of all people.

We believe that humans seek meaning in life and organize into religious communities to pursue meaning as a common endeavor. We believe that sexuality can enrich life and is thus an essential concern of religious communities. We recognize that people can encounter the spiritual through sexual expression.

Therefore, we believe the religious community must take an active role in the promotion of education and justice in human sexuality. To accomplish this, religious communities must engage in a wide range of activities and address the whole person through worshipping, nurturing, educating, supporting, challenging, advocating, confronting, forgiving, and healing.

This book is part of that effort. It will be a useful companion to positive and comprehensive lifespan educational programs that foster an awareness and experience of the integral relationship between spirituality and sexuality. One such program, *Our Whole Lives*, a lifespan curriculum for comprehensive sexuality education, is another joint endeavor of the Unitarian Universalist Association and the United Church Board for Homeland Ministries of the United Church of Christ. Designed for use in secular as well as religious settings, *Our Whole Lives* is intended to teach participants the knowledge, principles, and life skills they need to express their sexuality in life-enhancing ways.

The Advocacy Manual contains a variety of practical resources for introducing a comprehensive sexuality education program like *Our Whole Lives* in your congregation or community, as well as background information on sexuality education and its connection to spiritual and sexual health. Whether you are a parent, educator, student, clergyperson, or lay leader, we hope it will encourage you to employ your moral and religious values in advocating for comprehensive sexuality education. May this book be a launching pad for action in the service of justice, compassion, and equality.

> The Sexuality Education Task Force,
> The Unitarian Universalist Association and
> The United Church Board of Homeland Ministries

The Case for Comprehensive Sexuality Education

OVERVIEW

This book is a manual for advocates of comprehensive sexuality education programs in their religious and secular communities. An important first step in becoming an advocate is becoming informed about comprehensive sexuality education: its purpose, its underlying principles, and its differences from other forms of sexuality education. This overview and the other articles in this section will introduce the basics of comprehensive sexuality education and its alternatives.

Unless otherwise noted, quotations in this overview are taken from *Guidelines for Comprehensive Sexuality Education*, Second Edition, by the National Guidelines Task Force. These guidelines were composed by a group of teachers, public health professionals, social workers, and others representing many schools and other organizations across the US. The second edition of *Guidelines* was published in 1996 by the Sexuality Information and Education Council of the United States (SIECUS), a New York City-based organization that promotes sexuality programs.

WHAT IS COMPREHENSIVE SEXUALITY EDUCATION?

Comprehensive sexuality education understands sexuality as an essential part of every person, one that affects our identity, relationships, and intimacy throughout life. Comprehensive sexuality education thus does not limit itself to discussions of sexual feelings and acts, but usually discusses a wider range of topics, such as "sexual development, reproductive health, interpersonal relationships, affection, intimacy, body image, and gender roles."

Comprehensive sexuality education is comprehensive in terms of age. Although curricula vary, a truly comprehensive sexuality education program includes material for early elementary, later elementary, middle/junior high school, and high school students (and perhaps adults as well). Such material is presented in a developmentally appropriate manner. For example, while teenagers learn about the specifics of contraceptive use or sexually transmitted diseases, young children are taught the names of their body parts and what to do if an adult touches them in an inappropriate way.

Comprehensive sexuality education is comprehensive in its philosophy. Comprehensive sexuality education programs usually teach that, while most men and women are heterosexual, some are gay, lesbian, or bisexual; that while many teenagers and adults date, some do not; that there are different kinds of families and that families can change over time; that many teenagers have had sexual intercourse and many have not. In short, "a comprehensive sexuality education program respects the diversity of values and beliefs represented in the community."

Finally, comprehensive sexuality education is comprehensive in its goals. It does not intend merely to distribute information, but also to help students shape and articulate their values, build strong relationships, and learn to act responsibly. As stated in the *Guidelines*, the goals of comprehensive sexuality education can be summarized in four parts:

Information: To provide accurate information about human sexuality, including: growth and development, human reproduction, anatomy, physiology, masturbation, family life, pregnancy, childbirth, parenthood, sexual response, sexual orientation, contraception, abortion, sexual abuse, and HIV/AIDS and other sexually transmitted diseases.

Attitudes, Values, and Insights: To provide an opportunity for young people to understand and articulate their sexual attitudes in order to understand their family's values, develop their own values, increase self-esteem, develop insights concerning relationships with families and members of both genders, and understand their obligations and responsibilities to their families and others.

Relationships and Interpersonal Skills: To help young people develop interpersonal skills, including communication, decision-making, assertiveness, and peer refusal skills, as well as the ability to create satisfying relationships. Sexuality education programs should prepare students to understand their sexuality effectively and creatively in adult roles. This would include helping young people develop the capacity for caring, supportive, noncoercive, and mutually pleasurable intimate and sexual relationships when they become adults.

Responsibility: To help young people exercise responsibility regarding sexual relationships, including addressing abstinence, how to resist pressures to become prematurely involved in sexual intercourse, and encouraging the use of contraception and other sexual health measures. Sexuality education should be a central component of programs designed to reduce the prevalence of sexually related medical problems; these include teenage pregnancies, sexually transmitted diseases including HIV infection, and sexual abuse.

WHAT OTHER KINDS OF SEXUALITY EDUCATION EXIST?

Sexuality education programs offered in schools vary greatly in scope and quality. Some focus on the biological aspects of sexuality, others center on building skills to refuse sexual activity, others focus on delivering the knowledge and skills to make healthy decisions. Some discuss contraception and safer sex, and others do not. Schools often omit potentially controversial sexuality education topics, such as sexual identity, sexual orientation, masturbation, abortion, and sexuality and religion, leaving students to depend on other, often unreliable, sources for this information. A 1993 SIECUS study of state guidelines for sexuality education, *Unfinished Business*, indicated that "fewer than one-third of state guides include any sexual behavior topic other than abstinence."

It is important to draw a distinction between two predominant types of abstinence education: abstinence-based and abstinence-only. Abstinence-based programs focus on the benefits of abstinence from sexual activity, helping young people develop the skills they need to postpone sexual involvement. Abstinence-based programs also include information about contraception and preventing sexually transmitted diseases (STDs)—information that can help students make healthy decisions in the present and future. Comprehensive sexuality education programs can be abstinence-based.

Abstinence-only programs teach that abstinence from all sexual behaviors is the only acceptable option for unmarried people. These programs either make no mention of contraception and STD prevention or claim that birth control and condoms do not work. They emphasize the benefits of abstinence and the damaging effects of premarital sexual behavior. Only some abstinence-only programs acknowledge the existence of homosexuality. Those that do include homosexuality teach that gay and lesbian people should choose to remain celibate. Many of these programs are "fear-based," that is, they use fear of negative consequences as their major strategy to encourage premarital abstinence. Abstinence-only programs are promoted heavily by opponents of comprehensive sexuality education. These programs are frequently the source of intense community controversy.

Proponents of abstinence-only curricula often operate with the belief that parents find abstinence-only programs attractive and uncontroversial. In reality, the majority of parents support a more balanced approach to sexuality education—an approach that enables young people to make healthy choices by including information on abstinence, contraception, and STD prevention. The introduction of abstinence-only programs often invites controversy. This manual contains a case study about advocacy in Hemet, California, that profiles one such controversy. It can be found in the section called "In Your Community."

Because abstinence-only programs are strongly supported and promoted by organizations and individuals associated with the religious right, proponents of abstinence-only programs often further the mistaken assumption that all people of faith support an abstinence-only approach. Too frequently, advocates for comprehensive sexuality education have kept silent about their own religious values, leaving school boards and legislators to believe the religious right's claim that religious people oppose comprehensive sexuality education. In the midst of community controversy over abstinence-only programs, advocacy from people of faith who support comprehensive sexuality education is essential.

LEARNING MORE

This chapter contains additional articles about comprehensive sexuality education. "Sexuality Education and the Schools: Issues and Answers," a SIECUS fact sheet, offers additional information about school-based sexuality education and comprehensive sexuality education that is applicable to both congregation-based and school-based programs. "Philosophy: Comprehensive vs. Fear-Based Sexuality Education Programs," also provided by SIECUS, compares abstinence-only to comprehensive programs. Additional information on comprehensive sexuality education, as well as critiques of abstinence-only programs, can be obtained from SIECUS. Please see "Resources for More Information" in the Appendix.

Sexuality Education and the Schools:
Issues and Answers

Sexuality Information and Education Council of the United States

What is "sexuality education"?

Sexuality education is a lifelong process of acquiring information and forming attitudes, beliefs, and values about identity, relationships, and intimacy. It encompasses sexual development, reproductive health, interpersonal relationships, affection, intimacy, body image, and gender roles.[1]

How do people learn about sexuality?

Parents are the primary sexuality educators of their children. From the moment of birth, they teach children about love, touch, and relationships. Infants and toddlers receive the beginnings of sexuality education through example when their parents talk to them, dress them, show affection, and teach them the names of the parts of their bodies. As children grow, they continue to receive messages about appropriate behaviors and values as they develop relationships within their family and the social environment.

Children also learn about sexuality from sources outside their homes. Friends, teachers, neighbors, television, music, books, advertisements, and toys teach them about sexual issues.

The sexuality education that parents provide to their children can be supplemented by planned learning opportunities in churches, synagogues, and other places of worship, community and youth agencies, and schools.

Recent polls indicate that most young people look to their parents as their most important source of information about sexuality. Friends are the second most important source, school courses rank third, and television is fourth. More than two-thirds of young people have talked to their parents about sexuality.

Among the adults polled, a much smaller number learned about sexuality from their own parents (21 percent from the mother, 5 percent from the father), yet two-thirds of these adults have talked with their own children about sexual issues. In numerous studies, most parents report that they are uncomfortable discussing sexual issues with their children and welcome assistance from more formal programs.

Why school-based sexuality education?

School-based sexuality education programs conducted by specially trained educators can add an important dimension to children's ongoing sexual learning.

These programs should be developmentally appropriate and should include such issues as self-esteem, family relationships, parenting, friendships, values, communication techniques, dating, and decision-making skills.

Programs must be carefully planned by each community in order to respect the diversity of values and beliefs present in a classroom and community.

What are the goals of school-based sexuality education?

The primary goal of sexuality education is the promotion of adult sexual health. Sexuality education seeks to assist young people in understanding a positive view of sexuality, to provide them with information and skills about taking care of their sexual health, and to help them acquire skills to make decisions now and in the future.

Comprehensive sexuality education programs have four main goals:

- to provide accurate information about human sexuality;
- to provide an opportunity for young people to develop and understand their values, attitudes, and beliefs about sexuality;
- to help young people develop interpersonal skills; and
- to help young people exercise responsibility regarding sexual relationships, including addressing abstinence, how to resist pressures to become prematurely involved in sexual intercourse, and encouraging the use of contraception and other sexual health measures.[2]

Does the federal government require sexuality or HIV education?

There is no federal law or policy requiring sexuality or HIV education. Rather than dictating sexuality education and its content, the federal government has been explicit in its view that it should not control the content. While the statutes were not established solely in regard to sexuality education, four federal statutes preclude the federal government from prescribing state and local curriculum standards: the Department of Education Organization Act, Section 103a; the Elementary and Secondary Education Act, Section 14512; Goals 2000, Section 319(b); and the General Education Provisions Act, Section 438.

However, the welfare reform legislation signed in 1996 (Public Law 104-193) created a new federal entitlement program for abstinence-only education. Programs implemented as part of this initiative must have as their exclusive purpose teaching the "social, psychological, and health gains to be realized by abstaining from sexual activity" and cannot provide information about contraception or STD prevention.

Do states require sexuality or HIV education?

Twenty-three states and the District of Columbia require that schools provide sexuality education (AL, AR, DE, DC, FL, GA, HI, IL, IA, KS, MD, MN, NV, NJ, NM, NC, RI, SC, TN, TX, UT, VA, VT, WV).[3]

Thirty-seven states and the District of Columbia require schools to provide STD/HIV/AIDS education (AL, AR, CA, CT, DE, DC, FL, GA, HI, ID, IL, IN, IA, KS, MD, MI, MN, MO, NV, NH, NJ, NM, NY, NC, OH, OK, OR, PA, RI, SC, TN, TX, UT, VA, VT, WA, WV, WI).[4]

What should be included in school-based sexuality education?

The National Guidelines Task Force, composed of representatives from 15 national organizations, schools, and universities, has identified six key concept areas that should be part of any comprehensive sexuality education program. They are human development, relationships, personal skills, sexual behavior, sexual health, and society and culture. The National Guidelines Task Force issued *Guidelines for Comprehensive Sexuality Education* in October 1991, which include information on teaching 36 sexuality-related topics in an age-appropriate manner.[5] An updated edition of the *Guidelines* was published in 1996.

What is the content of sexuality education programs?

The content of sexuality education varies greatly depending on the community and the age level of the students in the program. The most commonly and thoroughly covered topics (in order) are body image, reproductive anatomy, puberty, decision-making skills, families, abstinence, STDs and HIV/AIDS, sexual abuse, and gender roles.[6]

Of the 26 states that require abstinence instruction, only 14 also require the inclusion of other information on contraception and pregnancy and disease prevention (AR, CA, DE, GA, IL, NC, OK, OR, RI, SC, TN, VT, VA, WA). [7]

Twenty-seven states and the District of Columbia require that schools provide family life education, such as child development, dating, explanation of family responsibilities, and interpersonal relationships (AL, AZ, AR, CA, CT, DE, DC, FL, GA, IL, IN, IA, LA, MD, MN, NV, NJ, NM, NC, OR, RI, SC, TN, TX, UT, VT, VA, WV).[8]

Thirty-one states and the District of Columbia require or recommend the inclusion of decision-making skills instruction, such as resisting peer pressure, setting limits during dates, teaching that it is wrong to make unwanted sexual advances, and encouraging personal responsibility and respect for others (AL, AZ, AR, CA, CO, DE, DC, FL, GA, IL, IA, LA, MD, MA, MN, MT, NV, NH, NJ, NM, NY, NC, OK, OR, RI, SC, TN, TX, UT, VT, VA, WV).[9]

Five states prohibit or restrict discussion of abortion (CT, IL, LA, MI, SC) and only Vermont and the District of Columbia require that discussions of abortion are included.[10]

Eight states require or recommend teaching that homosexuality is not an acceptable lifestyle and/or that homosexual conduct is a criminal offense under state law (AL, AZ, GA, LA, NC, SC, TX, VA), whereas one state (RI) requires that schools teach respect for others regardless of sexual orientation.[11]

Who decides the content of school-based sexuality education?

Many states have advisory committees. Thirty states have established a state school/community advisory committee to develop, review, or recommend appropriate sexuality education material and concepts taught at various grade levels.

These advisory committees reflect the recognition by states that programs are best developed with diverse input from external agencies and representatives. Such input also helps to develop community support for programs and to minimize negative reactions from sectors unfamiliar with programs.[12]

Is sexuality education effective?

Comprehensive approaches to sexuality education have been shown to be successful at helping young people postpone intercourse and use contraception and STD prevention.
     Research shows that effective programs:

- provide practice in communication, negotiation, and refusal skills;
- focus on reducing sexual behaviors that lead to unintended pregnancy or STDs;
- are based upon approaches that have been demonstrated effective in influencing other risky behaviors;
- provide basic and accurate information about methods of avoiding unprotected intercourse;
- use a variety of teaching methods to help students personalize information;
- are taught by trained teachers;
- include activities that address social and media pressures related to sex.[13]

An international study of sexuality education programs found that the best outcomes were obtained when education was provided prior to the onset of sexual activity and when information about abstinence, contraception, and STD prevention were included. The same study also found that sexuality education does not encourage sexual experimentation or increased activity.[14]

Do abstinence-only programs work?

Abstinence-only programs have not been found to be effective in helping young people to postpone sexual involvement. To date, six studies of abstinence-only programs have appeared in the scientific literature. None of these studies found consistent and significant program effects on delaying the onset of intercourse, and at least one study provided strong evidence that the program did not delay the onset of intercourse.
     Thus, the weight of the evidence indicates that abstinence-only programs do not delay the onset of intercourse.[15]

Can parents excuse their children from sexuality and HIV education?

Yes. Whether it is for sexuality education or HIV/AIDS education, states specifically provide parents with the option of removing their children from the classes or states defer to local decision makers to provide that option to parents. Nearly all local school districts have provisions for students opting out of sexuality education classes.[16] However, fewer than three percent of parents remove children from these educational programs.

Who supports sexuality education?

The vast majority of Americans support sexuality education. More than eight in ten parents want sexuality education taught in high schools.[17] Support for HIV/AIDS education is even higher. Ninety-four percent of parents think public schools should have an HIV/AIDS education program. More than eight out of ten parents want their children to be taught about safer sex as a way of preventing AIDS.[18]

Moreover, many youth, community, and national organizations have adopted policies supportive of sexuality education. More than 100 prominent national organizations have joined together as the National Coalition to Support Sexuality Education, a coalition of national organizations committed to assuring that all youth receive comprehensive sexuality education.

This SIECUS fact sheet, copyright © 1998, is reprinted with permission from the Sexuality Information and Education Council of the United States, 130 West 42nd Street, Suite 350, New York, New York 10036-7802.

SIECUS, the Sexuality Information and Education Council of the United States, is a national, nonprofit organization, incorporated in 1964, that promotes comprehensive education about sexuality and advocates the right of individuals to make responsible sexual choices.

REFERENCES

1. National Guidelines Task Force, *Guidelines for Comprehensive Sexuality Education, Kindergarten–12th Grade* (New York: SIECUS, 1991).
2. Ibid.
3. The NARAL Foundation, *Who Decides? A State-by-State Review of Abortion and Reproductive Rights* (Washington, DC: NARAL, 1997), p. xiii.
4. Ibid., p. xiv.
5. National Guidelines Task Force, *Guidelines for Comprehensive Sexuality Education, Kindergarten–12th Grade* (New York: SIECUS, 1991).
6. A. Gambrell and D. Haffner, *Unfinished Business: A SIECUS Assessment of State Sexuality Education Programs* (New York: SIECUS, 1993), p. 8.
7. The NARAL Foundation, *Sexuality Education in America: A State-by-State Review* (Washington, DC: NARAL, 1995), p. v.
8. Ibid., p. vi.
9. Ibid., p. vi.
10. Ibid., p. vi.
11. Ibid., p. vi.
12. A. Gambrell and D. Haffner, p. 14.
13. D. Kirby, *No Easy Answers: Research Findings on Programs to Reduce Teen Pregnancy* (Washington, DC: The National Campaign to Prevent Teen Pregnancy, 1997).
14. A. Grunseit and S. Kippax, *Effects of Sex Education on Young People's Sexual Behaviour* (Geneva: World Health Organization, 1993).
15. D. Kirby, *No Easy Answers: Research Findings on Programs to Reduce Teen Pregnancy* (Washington, DC: The National Campaign to Prevent Teen Pregnancy, 1997).
16. National Association for State Boards of Education, conversations with State Departments of Education, 1995.
17. Louis Harris and Associates, *America Speaks: Americans' Opinion on Teenage Pregnancy, Sex Education, and Birth Control* (New York: Planned Parenthood Federation of America, 1988), p. 24.
18. A. M. Gallup and D. L. Clark, *The 19th Annual Gallup Poll of the Public's Attitudes Toward the Public School* (New York: Gallup Polls, September 1987).

Philosophy:
Comprehensive vs. Fear-Based Sexuality Education Programs

Sexuality Information and Education Council of the United States

Comprehensive Sexuality Education Programs	Fear-Based, Abstinence-Only Programs
Focus	
• Views sexuality education as a lifelong process beginning at birth.	• Encourages abstinence from all sexual behaviors until marriage.
• Provides age-appropriate sexuality education throughout the school years.	• Offers limited information about sexual behavior.
• Includes information on a broad range of topics related to sexuality.	• Provides little or no information about contraception or safer sex.
• Emphasizes decision-making and critical-thinking skills.	• Does not introduce sexuality education until junior high.
Rationale	
• Sexuality education is a lifelong process that encompasses sexual development, reproductive health, interpersonal relationships, affection, intimacy, body image, and gender roles.	• A consistent and exclusive message of premarital abstinence is essential to outweighing media and peer pressure.
• Comprehensive sexuality education includes information about abstinence as well as about contraception and STD prevention.	• Contraceptive information in the classroom gives students a mixed message.

Comprehensive Sexuality Education Programs	Fear-Based, Abstinence-Only Programs
Goals	
• To provide accurate information about human sexuality.	• To promote premarital sexual abstinence.
• To give young people opportunities to identify their own values.	• To give young people the message that there is no acceptable premarital sexual behavior.
• To help young people develop interpersonal skills, including communication, decision-making, and refusal skills.	
• To help young people exercise responsibility regarding sexual relationships, including addressing abstinence and the use of contraception and other sexual health measures.	
Values	
• In a pluralistic society, people have different values and beliefs. Comprehensive sexuality education allows for the exploration of values which are shared in our society, as well as the exploration of values that may differ among individuals, communities, and families.	• Young people must learn core values of right and wrong sexual behavior.
Decision Making	
• Sexuality education can help young people develop decision-making skills by building critical-thinking skills, offering accurate information, and helping students examine their own values as well as the values of their families and the society at large.	• Values should not be based on the feelings or emotions of "autonomous," "decision-making" students. True values are standards of right action and moral necessity that are found outside the individual.
• Middle and late adolescents can make good decisions regarding sexuality, sexual behavior, and relationships.	• Young people cannot make decisions for themselves.

To obtain detailed reviews of specific fear-based curricula, contact the Sexuality Information and Education Council of the United States (SIECUS) at 130 West 42nd Street, Suite 350, New York, New York 10036-7802, 212/819-9770; or consult the SIECUS website at http://www.siecus.org.

Reprinted with permission from The SIECUS Community Action Kit: Information to Support Comprehensive Sexuality Education, *copyright © 1997 by the Sexuality Information and Education Council of the United States, 130 West 42nd Street, Suite 350, New York, New York 10036-7802.*

Religion and Sexuality

OVERVIEW

Asked about the relationship between religion and sexuality, many people would imagine two possibilities. In the first model, religion is critical of sexuality, seeing it as a worldly temptation that detracts from the virtuous life. In the second, religion and sexuality have nothing to do with each other at all.

But in some religious communities, in spiritual writings from many traditions, and in the minds of many who advocate for comprehensive sexuality education, sexuality is seen differently: as positive and special, a gift from God, an expression of the sacred, or a natural, healthy part of life. As Christian theologian James B. Nelson explains in his book *Between Two Gardens*, sexuality and spirituality are "inseparable elements of full personhood....The movement toward a more healed, wholistic spirituality and the movement to a more healed, wholistic sexuality cannot be separated. It is not just that they ought not to be separated; quite literally they cannot be."

Such a positive understanding of sexuality may well have been part of your religious experience, but it is not the norm. Many of us were raised to believe in a God that condemned any sexual activity (other than kissing) outside of heterosexual marriage. Many of us learned negative stereotypes about gay, lesbian, bisexual, and/or transgender people that were reinforced by our religious institutions. These ideas are common in our culture and in much of the public discourse surrounding sexuality education: so common, in fact, that they are sometimes taken to represent the sum total of religious perspectives on sexuality.

This false perception is abetted by religious communities that treat religion and sexuality as aspects of life that can be kept separate or compartmentalized. Many of us were raised to believe that sexuality and religion existed in separate realms—religion in the spirit and sexuality in the body. Wary of divisiveness and debate, some religious communities have understandably chosen to avoid discussing sexuality at all. But through their silence, these communities miss valuable opportunities to articulate different visions of sexuality and religious values, and to help their members develop the skills to evaluate sexual messages and make healthy decisions. Members want this help. In "Ask the Churches About Faith and Sexuality," a recent survey conducted by the United Church of Christ, 83 percent of members said they look to the church as a resource in sexuality-related decisions and concerns.

To do the work of sexuality education in our faith communities, and to advocate in secular settings as people of faith, it is helpful to understand both these entrenched perspectives and our own views of sexuality and faith. Perhaps you have come into this work as a sexuality education advocate because you have experienced healing and education

13

through your faith. Perhaps you have come into this work because you have experienced healing and education in spite of your faith. Perhaps your faith has evolved with you as you have done this work. And perhaps you are interested in learning about faith perspectives that understand sexuality in a more life-affirming way.

This section contains a number of resources for doing just that. The three essays that follow are reflections by individuals on sexuality, religion, and spirituality. "The Really Good News: What the Bible Says about Sex," by Debra W. Haffner, is a sexologist's fresh look at texts that are too often assumed to promote a negative and restrictive view of sexuality. Although one need not agree with Haffner's interpretations to do the work of sexuality education, it will be helpful for advocates in Christian and Jewish congregations and secular communities to be able to refer to biblical passages that describe sexuality in positive ways.

"Fidelity and Integrity: A Matter of Trust and Truth," by the Reverend Barbara Gerlach, and "Sex, Life, and Liberalism," by the Reverend Arthur S. Vaeni, are reflections on sexuality and faith by ministers of the United Church of Christ and the Unitarian Universalist Association, respectively. Their essays are included not because they represent the official theological standpoints of either denomination, but because they show how religious perspectives can inform our views of sexuality and sexuality education. (Information about the official positions taken by the Unitarian Universalist Association and the United Church of Christ can be found in the Appendix of this book.)

This section concludes with an annotated bibliography of books on sexuality and spirituality. Just as sexuality education is a lifelong process, so are religious education and spiritual development. The essays and books recommended can be starting points for personal and community exploration.

Faith-based advocates for sexuality education have the opportunity to promote healthier understandings of sexuality and religion and their relationship to one another. We hope the resources in this section will assist you in this task. The work of changing society *can* begin in our own communities, secular and religious, with each one of us.

The Really Good News:
What the Bible Says About Sex

Debra W. Haffner

During the past two years, I have become a serious student and avid reader of the Bible. I started my studies believing, as many adults with whom I have worked over the years believe, that the Bible either disparaged or ignored sexuality.

As I began my research last year as a Yale University Fellow, I discovered something quite different. Both the Hebrew Bible and the New Testament directly address sexuality issues and send messages that are quite different from what most people are taught in their religious groups and denominations. In fact, I now believe that a major function of Bible stories is to teach sexuality education: many of the stories and many of the laws contain information to help people understand the important role that sexuality plays in their lives.

Conversely, I was surprised to find that the Bible is absolutely silent about masturbation, abortion, birth control, oral-genital sex, and other sexual practices.

As I continued my work, I gradually realized that, by studying the Bible, readers can see how the people who created Scripture understood sexuality. And, in the process, they can also gain personal insights into the Bible's ability to speak to all of us today on these moral issues.

There is no question that certain church traditions have provided justification for sexual oppression. From the writings of Paul to those of Augustine and Aquinas—and through the current work of the Christian Coalition—parts of the Christian church have attempted to control, define, and limit sexual expression. In fact, it is clear that the mind/body dualism that characterizes much of Christian thought is the lens through which both the Bible and church traditions are used to limit people's experience of their sexuality and, indeed, to promote systematic oppression of sexuality.

However, these same theological tools can help demonstrate a revised sexual theology. Both scripture and church history are far richer on sexual issues than most people assume.

THE HEBREW BIBLE

The Hebrew Bible (also referred to as the Old Testament) is replete with stories that have sexual themes. Genesis itself has more than 30 stories that deal with sexual issues.

Genders and biological sex. The creation stories (Gen. 1 and 2) explain biological sex and the reasons for two genders. Genesis 1 says that God created "male and female, He created them" (Gen. 1:27) and then God blessed them: "Be fruitful and multiply" (Gen. 1:28). Genesis 2 is the more familiar telling of the creation of a woman from Adam's rib. God recognizes that "it is not good for man to be alone" (Gen. 2:18) and sets out to find Adam a companion. In fact, this solitariness is the first aspect of creation that God finds displeasing. Adam rejects all of the animals that God brings forward. It is only then that God puts Adam to sleep to create woman. The centrality of two genders and sexuality is emphasized: "Hence a man leaves his father and mother and clings to his wife and they become one flesh" (Gen. 2:24). According to these passages, man needs not only a companion and a helper but also a lover. The goal of union in Genesis 2:24 is sexual pleasure, not procreation. Side by side, the two creation texts reinforce that sexuality is both pro-creative and re-creative.

Sexual intercourse and desire. The importance of sexual intercourse and the role of desire appear numerous times in Genesis. Eve is told that despite the pain of childbirth, "your desire shall be for your husband" (Gen. 3:16). Divine beings were said to desire the beautiful human women (Gen. 6:2). Sarah describes sexual intercourse as "pleasure" (Gen. 18:12). Isaac is noticed "fondling his wife Rebekah" (Gen. 26:8). Leah and Rachel negotiate for Jacob's sexual favors (Gen. 30:14-16). Potiphar's wife strongly desires Joseph and asks him to sleep with her (Gen. 39:7). Intercourse itself is also frequently and publicly accounted for in Genesis: Adam "knew his wife Eve" (Gen. 4:1). "Cain knew his wife" (Gen. 4:17). "Adam knew his wife again" (Gen. 4:25). And so on.

Physical beauty and love at first sight. Physical beauty and love at first sight are also featured in Genesis. Rebekah "was very fair to look upon" (Gen. 24:16). Rachel "was graceful and beautiful" (Gen. 29:17). Joseph was "handsome and good looking" (Gen. 39:6). Jacob and Rachel fall in love at first sight (Gen. 29) and he happily waits seven years to marry her: "they seemed to him but a few days because of the love he had for her" (Gen. 29:20). Rebekah assuaged Isaac's grief after the death of Sarah: "He loved her. So Isaac was comforted after his mother's death" (Gen. 24:67).

Fertility. Fertility is referred to in Genesis as a gift from God. God's first words to people are "be fruitful and multiply" (Gen. 1:28). However, the matriarchs of the Hebrew Bible are all initially infertile: "God chose three infertile women and one woman [Leah] who was not desirable to her husband to bear children who would inherit the covenant."[1] God's direct intervention helps these women to conceive. Sarah has her son at 90 after lifelong infertility (Gen. 21:2). God healed Abimelech's "wife and his female slaves so that they bore children" (Gen. 20:17); God resolved Rebekah's infertility (Gen. 25:21); "[t]he Lord saw that Leah was unloved, he opened her womb; but Rachel was barren" (Gen. 29:31); but eventually "God remembered Rachel; and God heeded her and opened her womb" (Gen. 30:22). The Hebrew Bible also recounts two stories where infertile women arrange for their husbands to have children with other women: Sarah sends Abraham to have sex with Hagar (Gen. 16:2), and Rachel tells Jacob to "go in to" her maid Bilhah so that she may have children through her (Gen. 30:3).

Genitals and bodily functions. Genesis also speaks directly about genitals and bodily functions. God asks the ancients to "circumcise the flesh of your foreskins" as the "sign of the covenant between me and you" (Gen. 17:11). Circumcision assures that the "covenant be in your flesh an everlasting covenant" (Gen. 17:13). In 1970, theologian and marriage counselor David Mace wrote that the penis was chosen for this mark because it was the most holy part of the body: "It was with this special organ that he became, in a special sense, a coworker with God."[2]

It also speaks frankly about menstruation. The writers knew that the end of menses was likely to be the end of fertility (Gen. 18: 11). Menstruation is actually used as a plot device in the story of Rachel's deception of Laban (Gen. 31:32-35).

Destructive uses of sexuality. Genesis also contains numerous warnings about the potentially destructive uses of sexuality. There are references to rape (Gen. 34:1-4), gang rape (Gen. 19:4-8), incest (Gen. 19:31-39), and prostitution (Gen. 38:15-17). In the three versions of the wife/sister stories, Abraham and Isaac try to pass their wives off as their sisters and almost endanger peace in the land (Gen. 12, 26, and 20).

The Bible does not, however, contain the negative sexual messages that people assume. For example, Sodom and Gomorrah is *not* a story against consensual same-gender sexual relations. Rather, the sin is about inhospitality and gang rape. Likewise, the sin of Onan is not about masturbation but about his ignoring the Levirate Law to procreate with his dead brother's wife. Onan does not masturbate to avoid procreation. He practices coitus interruptus: but "Onan knew that the offspring would not be his, he spilled his semen on the ground whenever he went in to his brother's wife" (Gen. 38:9), something he apparently did with some frequency.

Sexuality in relationships. The special role of sexuality in the first year of a sexual relationship is underscored in Deuteronomy in this translation from the Tanakh: "When a man has taken a bride, he shall not go out with the army or be assigned to it for any purpose; he shall be exempt for one year for the sake of his household, to give happiness to the woman he has married" (Deut. 24:5). (Writing about this passage in the 16th century, Martin Luther wrote that it is "as though Moses wanted to say, 'The joy will last for a year; after that we shall see.'"[3]) Proverbs also contains hope for ongoing sexual intimacy in a long-term relationship: "Let your fountain be blessed, and rejoice in the wife of your youth, a lovely deer, a graceful doe. May her breasts satisfy you at all times; may you be intoxicated always by her love" (Prov. 5:18-19).

Same-gender sexual relations. The Bible contains only four verses about same-gender sexual relations: two in Leviticus and two in the New Testament. Leviticus says that "you shall not lie with a male as with a woman; it is an abomination" (Lev. 18:22), and "if a man lies with a male as with a woman, both of them have committed an abomination; they shall be put to death; their blood is upon them" (Lev. 20:13). The same scripture says that cursing your mother and father is also punishable by death (Lev. 20:9) as is sex with the wife of a neighbor (Lev. 20:10), one's father's wife (Lev. 20:11), daughter-in-law (Lev. 20:12), both a woman and her mother (Lev. 20:14), or an animal (Lev. 20:15-16). Other acts punishable by exile according to Leviticus are seeing family members naked and having sex during menstruation (Lev. 20:17-21).

In the New Testament, the opening passages of Romans condemn pagan practices. The book then denounces sex with someone of the same gender: "For this reason God gave them up to degrading passions. Their women exchanged natural intercourse for un-natural" (Rom. 1:26), "and in the same way, also the men, giving up natural intercourse with women, were consumed with passion for one another. Men committed shameless acts with men and received in their own persons the due penalty for their error" (Rom. 1:27). In addition, verses in 1 Corinthians 6:9-10 and 1 Timothy 1:10 equate "fornica-tors, idolators, adulterers, male prostitutes, and sodomites" with other sinners such as the "greedy, drunkards, revilers, robbers" (1 Cor. 6:9-10). But these two books never offer definitions for these terms.

It is, at best, inaccurate to use scripture to condemn committed, consensual same-gender sexual relationships. The fact that only four verses explicitly address this issue im-plies that this subject was of relatively little importance to the authors. In contrast, there are more than ten prohibitions in Leviticus against sexual relations during menses and 17 verses on how to make a grain offering. The Hebrew Bible also condemns eating fat (Lev. 3:17), touching the bedding of a menstruating woman (Lev. 15:20), and cursing one's parents (Lev. 20:9, Deut. 21:18-21).

Most modern theologians believe that these passages about men having sex with men actually related to the rejection of nearby foreign cults (Lev. 20:22-23). Such cults practiced sacred prostitution—often using male prostitutes—during religious obser-vances. Prostitution was an accepted part of urban society during biblical times (see 1 Kings 22:38, Isa. 23:16, Prov. 7:12 and 9:14); cultic prostitution (or prostitution as part of religious practice) was, however, clearly condemned. Deuteronomy and Numbers con-tain several prohibitions against such prostitution (Deut. 23:18 and Num. 25:1-3) but none on same-gender relations. Many theologians believe that Leviticus refers only to the use of male sacred prostitutes, a practice not completely eradicated in the Temple until the reforms of Josiah (1 Kings 15:12, 22:45; 2 Kings 23:7)[4]

Interestingly, there are several little quoted passages in the Bible that acknowledge sexual contact and love between men. For example, Abraham asks his servant to swear an oath by putting "your hand under my thigh" (Gen. 24:2). David, speaking of Jonathan, wrote: "...greatly beloved were you to me, your love to me was wonderful, passing the love of women" (2 Sam. 1:26). Indeed, Jonathan and David seem to fall in love at first sight: "...when David had finished speaking to Saul, the soul of Jonathan was bound to the soul of David, and Jonathan loved him as his own soul" (1 Sam. 18:1). And later, "Saul's son Jonathan took great delight in David" (1 Sam. 19:1).

Adultery. The Bible clearly condemns adultery. It is important to understand, how-ever, that adultery is looked upon not as a sexual sin but as a violation of property rights. In Biblical times, adultery was defined as having sex with another man's wife or concu-bine without his permission, not as having sex outside of one's marriage. Indeed, Proverbs 6:26 urges men to seek prostitutes, whose fee is equal only to a loaf of bread, rather than be tempted by the wife of another. People in biblical times felt that a man who committed adultery was not violating his own marriage, but rather that of the other woman and her husband. During the period in which the New Testament was written, the husband was said to commit adultery if he divorced his wife (Matt. 5:32, Mark 10:11, and Luke 16:18), and it was forbidden in several books (Rom. 13:9, Gal. 5:19, and James 2:11).

There are few restraints on men and sex in the Leviticus and Deuteronomy codes besides adultery. For example, there is no limit on the number of wives and concubines that a man could have (Solomon was said to have 700 wives and 300 concubines) (1 Kings 11:3), and male virginity is not discussed. The law is silent on sexual behavior for an engaged couple.

Celibacy. Celibacy is never presented positively in the Hebrew Bible. During the disorganized period of time in Judges, Jephthah's daughter begs her father for two months' reprieve before she is to die because she is still a virgin: "grant me two months, so that I may go and wander on the mountains, and bewail my virginity, my companions and I" (Judg. 11:37). The daughters of Israel went out each year to mourn Jephthah's daughter because "she had never slept with a man" (Judg. 11:39). Similarly, the prophet Jeremiah remained single as an example of the disorganization that characterized Israel at that time (Jer. 16:2).

The Song of Solomon. The most overtly sexual book of the Bible are the Canticles or the Song of Solomon. Throughout history, there have been attempts to understand the Song of Solomon as an allegory. In various books, the Song is described as a book about the love of God for Israel, or about the love of Jesus for the church, or even about historical battles. Modern scholars have, by and large, dismissed these interpretations, believing that they "do not explicate the primary level of the text, which is explicitly about human love and nowhere mentions God."[5] The Song of Solomon celebrates erotic love between a man and a woman in a remarkably mutual relationship. Marcia Falk in the Harper's Bible Commentary says that "women speak as assertively as men, initiating action at least as often; men are free to be as gentle, as vulnerable, even as coy as women. Men and women similarly praise each other for their sensuality and their beauty, and identical phrases are sometimes used to describe lovers of both genders."[6]

The Song does not talk about sex in the context of marriage or procreation: the woman in the Song is never "called a wife, nor is she required to bear children. In fact, to the issue of marriage and procreation, the Song does not speak."[7]

The Song is remarkably explicit in its erotic descriptions. Consider, for example, these two passages:

> My beloved thrust his hand into the opening,
> and my inmost being yearned for him.
> I arose to open to my beloved,
> and my hand dripped with myrrh,
> my fingers with liquid myrrh. . . .(Song of Sol. 5:4-5).

> How fair and pleasant you are
> O loved one, delectable maiden!
> You are stately as a palm tree
> and your breasts are like its clusters.
> I say I will climb the palm tree
> and lay hold of its branches.
> Oh, may your breasts be like
> clusters of the vine,

and the scent of your breath like apples,
and your kisses like the best wine
that goes down smoothly
gliding over lips and teeth. (Song of Sol. 7:6-9)

Interestingly, after Genesis and Psalms, the Song was the most frequently expounded book of the Old Testament in the middle ages. Denys Turner in *Eros and Allegory* observes this irony: "male celibates, priests, and monks have for centuries described, expressed, and celebrated their love of God in the language of sex."[8]

Some early theologians warned against the text: Denys the Carthusian, for example, warned that the Song should not be read by anyone under 30, and that only people who are "reformed, purified of sensual desire" will not be harmed by its reading. Giles of Rome said that "the text here seems to be defective."[9]

The Latter Prophets present a much more daunting picture of marriage and sexuality. The marriage metaphors of Hosea, Jeremiah, and Ezekiel all portray relationships gone awry: "Plead with your mother, plead—for she is not my wife and I am not her husband..." (Hos. 2:2). "...I will hedge up her way with thorns and I will build a wall against her, so that she cannot find her paths" (Hos. 2:6). In these passages, Israel is portrayed as the adulterous wife and God as the husband who has deserted her.

Even in the times surrounding the exile, however, the love between men and women are still held as an ideal. For example, in Jeremiah, the Lord says to Israel, "I am going to banish from this place, in your days and before your eyes, the voice of mirth and the voice of gladness, the voice of the bridegroom and the voice of the bride." Numerous analogies related to sexual abuse, rape, and adultery are used to indicate the coming destruction.

The promise of God to Israel is referred to in terms of intimate relationships. Consider this passage from Isaiah:

...but you shall be called My Delight Is In Her
and your land Married.
For the Lord delights in you,
and your land shall be married.
For as a young man marries a young woman,
so shall your builder marry you,
and as the bridegroom rejoices over the bride;
so shall your God rejoice over you (Isa. 62:4-5).

This passage is reminiscent of the passage in Deuteronomy previously quoted; the special relationship of a couple newly in love is celebrated. The prophets recognized that a righteous relationship between a man and a woman is as holy as God's love for Israel.

THE NEW TESTAMENT

The New Testament includes little discussion of sexuality issues. However, The First Letter of Paul to The Church at Corinth (also known as 1 Corinthians) is rich in such coverage. In fact, it contains many of the topics in current sexuality education programs and can be viewed as a form of sexuality instruction for the first century.

First Corinthians includes some coverage of at least 17 sexuality topics. In his letter, Paul briefly addresses anatomy, families, child-rearing, values, decision making, communication, assertiveness, shared sexual behavior, and sexual desire. He also provides extensive information on bodies, love, marriage, gender roles, sexuality and society, law, and religion. First Corinthians recognizes the sacredness of the body and sexual relationships, reinforces that sexual desire is part of life, and respects the importance of mutual and egalitarian pleasure and responsibility in intimate relationships. It also affirms marriage and presents a brilliant description of love.

Paul believed that the "body is a temple of the Holy Spirit" (1 Cor. 6:19). He also recognized the sacredness of all parts of the body: "God arranged the members in the body, each one of them, as he chose. If all were a single member, where would the body be? As it is, there are many members, yet one body" (1 Cor. 12:18-20). Although he unfortunately differentiated between more and less honorable parts of the body, he asserted that "...there may be no dissension within the body, but the members may have the same care for one another" (1 Cor. 12:25).

Paul underscored that sexual relations are sacred and not to be engaged in lightly. First Corinthians 6:12-20 should not be read as condemning all sexual relationships as some theologians have implied. Rather, it affirms that sexuality has the ability to profoundly affect one's life. Many scholars have written that *porneia* should not be translated as fornication but rather as *sexual immorality as delineated by the Torah*.[10] Paul was urging Christians to avoid using prostitutes—especially cultic prostitutes—because the physical act of intercourse involves the sanctity of becoming "one flesh." In the words of William Countryman, Paul "regarded sexual desire as a natural appetite, though one too central to human identity to be treated casually."[11] Paul recognized that adults experience sexual desire. He felt that people have the ability to make decisions about their sexual feelings, that sexual feelings are not uncontrollable, and that they should be acknowledged and acted upon only as they support one's values (1 Cor. 7:36-38).

Paul did not suggest abstinence and celibacy for all. He believed that permanently abstaining from sexual relationships is a special gift: "I wish that all were as I myself am. But each has a particular gift from God, one having one kind and another a different kind" (1 Cor. 7:7). Indeed, in a surprising admission, he stated that his personal belief in celibacy was not from Jesus or God: "Now concerning virgins, I have no command of the Lord" (1 Cor. 7:25).

Paul clearly affirmed marriage as the context for sexual relationships and emphasized the mutuality of roles. "The husband should give to his wife her conjugal rights, and likewise the wife to the husband. For the wife does not have authority over her own body; but the husband does. Likewise, the husband does not have authority over his own body; but the wife does" (1 Cor. 7:3-5).

Further, partners have a right to expect sexual relations on a regular basis: "Do not deprive one another except perhaps by agreement for a set time" (1 Cor. 7:5).

Paul wavered in his understanding of the equality of both genders, but he did underscore the unique contributions of both. Although there are certainly lines in this text that are overtly patriarchal (1 Cor. 11:8-10), other verses recognize the importance of both genders: "in the Lord woman is not independent of man or man independent of woman" (1 Cor. 11:11).

The centrality of the message of love is a basic component of all good sexuality education programs. And here, Paul is as relevant today as he was two millennia ago. Chapter 13 could be a central point of study for sexuality education programs from adolescence to adulthood:

> Love is patient; love is kind; love is not envious or boastful or arrogant or rude.... It bears all things, believes all things, hopes all things, endures all things. (1 Cor. 13:4-7)

TOWARD A NEW SEXUAL THEOLOGY

Numerous religious denominations are struggling with sexuality issues, and the Bible is an important place to start these explorations. Jewish and Christian individuals who are seeking to understand the role that sexuality plays in their lives can look to Scripture for insights and understanding.

Without a doubt, there is an urgent need for a new sexual theology that will help people recognize the value of sexuality. Theologian James Nelson has eloquently stated the goals of such a theology:

> It will be strongly sex-affirming, understanding sexual pleasure as a moral good rooted in the sacred value of our sensuality and erotic power, and not needing justification by procreative possibility. It will be grounded in respect for our own and other's bodily integrity and will help us defend against the common sexual violations of that integrity. It will celebrate fidelity in our commitments without legalistic prescription as to the precise forms such fidelity must make. It will be an ethic whose principles apply equally and without double standards to persons of both genders, of all colors, ages, bodily conditions, and sexual orientations.[12]

To that, I add, "Amen." Sexologists need to take a new look at the Bible and its influence on many of the people we serve. We need to understand that the Bible teaches that sexuality is a central part of being human, that bodies are good, that pleasure is good, and that men and women experience a healthy desire of each other.

Just as it is today, sexuality in biblical times was a source of pleasure and intimacy as well as misery and distress. Bible stories and passages can help people identify and live according to their own values and to discriminate between sexual decisions that are life-enhancing or destructive. Those of us who are people of faith must spread the gospel, literally the "good news," that the Bible affirms a healthy and positive view of sexuality.

Author's note: I am grateful to the Yale Divinity School for the opportunity to participate in their Fellowship program and to its faculty for its assistance in my studies.

Rev. Debra W. Haffner is co-founder and director of the Religious Institute.

REFERENCES

1. S. P. Jeansonne, *Women of Genesis* (Minneapolis: Fortress Press, 1990).
2. D. R. Mace, *The Christian Response to the Sexual Revolution* (New York: Abington Press, 1970).
3. *Luther's Works*, vol. 28 (St. Louis: Concordia Publishing House, 1973), p. 12.
4. L. M. Epstein, *Sex Laws and Customs in Judaism* (New York: Block Publishing Company, 1948).
5. M. Falk, "Song of Songs," *Harpers Bible Commentary* (San Francisco: Harper and Row, 1988).
6. Ibid.
7. P. Trible, *God and the Rhetoric of Sexuality* (London: SCM Press Ltd, 1978).
8. D. Turner, *Eros and Allegory* (Kalamazoo, Mich.: Cistercian Publications, 1995).
9. Ibid.
10. R. Lawrence, *The Poisoning of Eros* (New York: Augustine Moore Press, 1989).
11. L. W. Countryman, *Dirt, Greed, and Sex* (Philadelphia: Fortress Press, 1988).
12. J. B. Nelson, *Body Theology* (Louisville, Ky.: Westminster/John Knox Press, 1992), p. 21.

Fidelity and Integrity:
A Matter of Trust and Truth

Rev. Barbara Gerlach

Growing up in my home, the "sin above all sins" was having sex before marriage. My mother was terrified that one of her daughters would get pregnant and not go on to college. We were cautioned on the dangers of necking and petting. We were drilled on the double standard because boys' sexual drives were stronger, and it was up to us girls to hold the line. Now I give my mother credit. She was determined that her daughters would know more about sex than she learned from her mother. But there were some glaring gaps, like how to navigate all that sexual and relational water between that first goodnight kiss and the wedding night.

It's that difficult sexual and relational water that I would like to reflect on here. And it doesn't end on the wedding night or with the decision to remain single. There's nothing like strong sexual feelings to set us in turmoil at any stage of life, no matter what our sexual preference or marital status.

A little over a year ago, the Presbyterian Church passed a resolution on chastity and fidelity: chastity in singleness, fidelity in marriage between a man and a woman. But the resolution reflected more than a desire to set sexual standards. It was an attempt to keep homosexuals, including those in committed relationships, out of the ordained leadership of the church.

When a similar resolution was brought to the United Church of Christ General Synod this summer, it underwent a transformation and resulted in a resolution that celebrated the diverse relationships in which covenant and commitment, fidelity and integrity are essential and foundational. It reaffirmed fidelity and integrity as the standard for sexual and relational behavior in marriage and in other covenanted relationships, but also in singleness and in all relationships of life.

My colleague Jim Ross tells of a conversation he had this summer with his 15-year-old granddaughter Cathy, who asked him, "How do you know when you're in love?" Jim answered, "You know you're in love, because you can't think of anybody else. That person becomes your whole world." This is the obsessional stage of love, when love is new and exciting and all-consuming.

It's wonderful when this obsession is mutual, and when both people are single and free to fall in love, and when their love matures into a committed, lifelong relationship. But what Jim didn't tell Cathy is that love is usually a lot more emotionally and decisionally complicated. Complicated because sometimes the person you are obsessed with isn't interested in you and your love goes unrequited. Complicated because the passion of the moment can cause us to do impulsive things, like one-night stands, or lying and sneaking around, or unsafe sex and someone gets pregnant or AIDS or hurt or used. Complicated because one or both of the people are already in a committed relationship and what do you do with those feelings then?

Complicated because, even while some of us long for love, we don't have much luck or opportunity or success in finding the right person and developing a relationship. Complicated because even if we are single by choice or are alone again because our partner dies or leaves, we still have needs, sexual and relational needs for physical touch and intimacy. Complicated because even in the best of marriages, the falling in love stage passes, passions ebb and flow, and we are faced with the challenge of fidelity: How do we stay in love and renew our relationships?

It seems to me that sexual love has two poles, passion and faithfulness. We long for both, but at times they pull in opposite directions. The passionate side of love can be both wonderful and dangerous and that's why we put fences around it and have rules, like thou shalt not commit adultery or no sex before marriage or sex belongs within the context of a loving committed relationship. As long as there are human beings, there will be people who accept the collective wisdom and abide within the community's sexual standard, and there will be others who break the rules and scale the fences and have to learn, sometimes painfully or destructively, from their own experience.

I have a friend who reflected with me on a special, but not quite consummated, relationship with a woman outside of his marriage. He said it was like this group of different churches in some distant land that gathered and celebrated communion together while their leaders were away. Afterwards they decided, "It was the most wonderful thing that ever happened. And it will never happen again."

Because we break the sexual rules or feel ambivalent about them, that doesn't mean there shouldn't be any rules at all, or any values and visions we hold up as standards for our personal behavior, or any values and visions we affirm as foundational for the well-being of our community. It's important to come up with values that communities can agree upon and use to guide their relationships, even when we know that our social consensus sometimes shifts and changes, and there will always be followers and breakers of the rules.

For instance, I suspect most of us would agree that infidelity is bad because it breaks trust and undermines loving, committed relationships. We would also agree that fidelity for fidelity's sake when a relationship has become dead, destructive, or loveless can also be bad, so there is a place for divorce in our sexual ethic. We would also probably agree that we don't want our children and teenagers having sex too young before they are mature enough to make decisions about safe, responsible, and loving relationships.

It's just that within the religious spectrum, there are those who believe the Bible sets clear and absolute rules for sexuality, such as chastity in singleness and fidelity in heterosexual marriage. There are others who come to their sexual and relational decisions out of a more fluid interplay between individual conscience, their family's values, and the visions received from their faith community. These faith communities weigh not only what the Bible says, but principles such as mutual trust and responsibility; honesty, justice, and health; age-level appropriateness; cultural differences; and recent insights from science and psychology.

It seems to me that there are three dynamics important in making our sexual decisions: truth, trust, and talking together.

First, it's a matter of truth. We have to listen for our truth out of the depths of our experience and conscience, and risk speaking that truth in love, even when our truth seems different from that of those we love. Isn't that part of what integrity is? Speaking our whole truth? Bringing our whole being to our relationships? If we don't make ourselves known, then we can never feel truly loved. But we also have to listen to the truth of others, because our truth is partial and self-centered and needs to be modified and broadened by the perspectives of others. But more than listening to the truth of our little circle of family and friends and church, or our own time or culture, we also have to listen to the collected wisdom of the past, which reflects the best thinking of those who have gone before us on sexual and relational matters. At the same time, we have to be open to new truth, to the sense that God isn't finished with us yet and creation continues, and new light is always breaking forth on our sexual and relational ethic. For most of us that has happened around homosexuality. There has been a great change between what we thought 25 or 30 years ago and what we think now as gays and lesbians have come out and made themselves known. Finally we have to judge our truth by our actions, by the impact and consequences they have on others. Are our actions loving or destructive? Do they break down or build up relationships?

Second, it's a matter of trust. Trust is very close to truth. There is no trust without truth; what you see is what you get. One of the worst experiences for some of my divorced friends was not being able to see the breakup coming. Dissatisfactions were hidden, feelings were withheld, a lover kept secret. One of the things that has helped me with my sexual decision-making is imagining what I would feel if my husband John did what I was considering. Would I be hurt, my trust undermined, my confidence in our love threatened? We have to put ourselves in one another's shoes, which can be difficult when we are obsessed. And finally I ask, "Would I want others to know?" The breaking of trust between two partners has a larger ripple effect. Anyone who goes to see the movie *Eve's Bayou* will see the effect of the husband's infidelities, not only on his wife and the other woman and her husband, but most especially on the children, in their confusion and anger and the sexualizing of their relationship with their father to win his love. In our deepest committed love, we need to feel some things are sacred, special, unique, and exclusive to our relationship. But we need more than sexual fidelity. We also need a special emotional intimacy as part of the wholeness and integrity of our love.

Finally, it's a matter of talk. Poet Adrienne Rich wrote a book and an essay called "Lies, Secrets, and Silence." We all know about hiding and withholding, avoiding and deceiving in our deepest relationships. We want the people we love to read our minds and sense our deepest need, so we don't have to risk revealing ourselves. Truth and trust involve talking, making ourselves known to the one we love, but also talking with our communities of faith. As a teenager, I remember my terror of uttering any of my sexual dilemmas in church for fear of someone saying, "You did what?" and being judged for some great sexual transgression. Today in our much more sexually permissive culture, there is probably a greater fear of being ridiculed for the lack of sexual experience. Talking together, we realize that we are all uncertain about things sexual and relational. Falling and staying in love are hard to do. It's hard to be true to ourselves and true to others. It's hard to keep our passion and faithfulness together.

Gayle McFarland, at her recent ordination council, observed that covenants are more important than creeds and confessions in the United Church of Christ, and that joining a church is making a covenant to be part of a community. She said that our covenant to walk together reads almost like wedding vows, except that it is a covenant to be part of a community rather than between two people and God. We commit to be faithful to this particular community of people, where we can seek the truth, speak our truth, and trust that we will find people with whom we can walk and talk together. We are called to fidelity and integrity, not only in singleness and our committed relationships, but in all the relationships in our lives.

The Reverend Barbara Gerlach is an artist and is on the ministry staff of the First Congregational United Church of Christ in Washington, DC. Her essay is an edited version of a sermon preached to that congregation on November 23, 1997.

Sex, Life, and Liberalism

Rev. Arthur S. Vaeni

On a recent visit to the Botanical Gardens in Washington, DC, I found more varieties of orchids than I ever had seen before in one place. Now the orchid is quite an extraordinary plant, to the particular beauty of which I was introduced by my wife, Sally, a gardener extraordinaire. It's such an enticing flower, with coloring so lovely, forms so smooth, sensuous, and suggestive that it has the power to evoke a wonderfully sensual response. I'm sure the plant doesn't have the same effect on everyone. But that it does evoke such a response from some doesn't speak so much to the characteristics of the plant necessarily as it does to our innate human characteristics—our sensuousness and our sexuality. We are sensuous beings; that is, we are affected by the world through our senses. Sensations of touch, taste, sight, smell, and hearing flow into our being, into our awareness. We know we are alive. We are within and of this world, this life.

We are likewise sexual beings. Many of us experience our most intimate relationships through the expression of our sexuality. Our sexual energy is a powerful force that can intimate that sense of life's oneness, even as it can likewise wreak havoc in one's life. What's curious is that given its significance in our lives, so many of us wish to pretend that it isn't a part of who we are.

If it was simply that we denied our sexuality, that would be bad enough, but what is truly unfortunate is the underlying cultural belief that sex is bad, that experiencing oneself as a sexual being is usually sinful. It may seem ironic for that to be so, given the prevalence of sex as a commodity in our society, but it's not ironic at all. One of life's truths I've discerned is that when we deny that which is an important part of who we are, it still has a way of finding expression, usually in some distorted or even perverse manner. In general, as a society we've sought to deny that we are sexual beings. How did that come to be?

On one of the other days I spent in Washington, I came upon an amazing structure I had never heard of before, the Basilica of the National Shrine of the Immaculate Conception. It's a huge, striking church built in the beginning of the twentieth century. When I looked up at one of the supporting arches near the front of the church, I saw a depiction of two women, one with her head bowed in shame and the other radiant in her glory. The caption over them read: "Eve brought death; Mary brought life." In that moment I experienced a sense of sadness mixed with anger. How much harm has come from that belief?

The creation stories in the book of Genesis have had a powerful impact upon the Western notions of the human experience and qualities. And one particular interpretation of those stories by the Christian bishop Augustine held sway in the Church since the fifth or sixth centuries. It had long been understood up until Augustine, in both the

Jewish and Christian traditions, that the transgression of Adam and Eve had been the cause of human mortality.

But others felt that Adam and Eve's progeny retained the capacity to redeem themselves. Augustine said no. That original sin had been passed through the transmission of Adam's corrupted seed from generation to generation. His view wasn't automatically accepted by other theologians of his time. He was challenged and in one exchange he was asked, "What is nature?" As part of his response, he replied that mortality and sexual desire are not natural, but entered the human experience only to punish Adam's sin. Spontaneous sexual desire is both the proof and the penalty of original sin. Lust is not subject to control by the human will. Before Adam and Eve's fall from grace, he maintained, they could control their desire, and their decision whether or not to engage in sex could be equated to deciding to shake hands—and presumably with no more passion than that entails. It's no wonder Eden was so peaceful.

Of course, our primal parents fell from grace before Augustine's theory could be put to the test. Augustine proposed that we are naturally ashamed of our sexual desire, which is why we cover our genitals and shield intercourse from public view. In his view we should be ashamed, for our sexuality is both the proof of and the penalty for our innate sinfulness.

So how did his view—a view that was not shared by many other prominent theologians of his time—win such widespread acceptance in the following generations? Who knows? In part, perhaps, because it was tied in with his notion that original sin had cost us our moral freedom. At a time when life felt unsafe in the disintegrating Roman Empire, it may have helped people think they understood what was going on. In response to the perennial question, "Why do bad things happen?," the answer is provided: Bad things happen because people are innately sinful. It often seems true that we're so desperate for explanations—we can't tolerate the possibility that we may be subject to random violence—that we would rather believe we are guilty of some unknown transgression than believe that life may not always have reasons.

There's a joke from the *New Yorker* in which an apparently nervous man appears before St. Peter and the Pearly Gates. With a look of bemusement, St. Peter says, "No, no, that's not a sin either. My goodness, you must have worried yourself to death." Well, however it happened, Augustine's understanding of human sexuality prevailed and has been ingrained into the American cultural ethic as well as into our shared consciousness. As I mentioned earlier, I believe that's in large measure why sex is so prominent in American society and often in such destructive ways. In Jungian terms I would say that sex is part of our cultural shadow. So how do we get it out of the shadow? The liberal response—liberal as in, "of or befitting a free person, broadminded"—calls us to seek an understanding of our sexuality, to understand it as part of our humanity.

Heeding that call more than 25 years ago, Unitarian Universalists developed a sexuality education program named *About Your Sexuality*. About 12 years ago, when I first took the training to lead the program, I realized that I had made it into my late thirties without ever having been in a situation in which I could thoughtfully explore my conceptions about sex, sexuality, or even intimacy. The only sex education I had ever experienced occurred in my Catholic high school during a two-day sex education lecture. There I learned such helpful things as it being okay to French kiss before marriage if both parties were in separate tubs of ice water. In fairness that was said somewhat tongue-in-cheek, but it still conveys a fairly representative idea of the nature of the program. Sex education wasn't intended to help us understand ourselves as sexual beings, but to ensure we understood the narrow limits of acceptable behavior.

That's what makes programs like *About Your Sexuality* and the new *Our Whole Lives* different. It's not so much about defining those clear boundaries, which makes a lot of us adults uneasy because that's all we know, as it's about providing information and a safe, open forum for discussion about human sexuality so that our young people can make wise and moral decisions regarding relationships. I believe that such education is among the most significant and wonderful offerings we have made, and can make, toward the healthy development of our youth.

Sexuality is intrinsic to the human experience. Hiding from it serves only to make us vulnerable to its misuse as a source of power over, rather than power with, others. It's quite clear we can abuse our own and others' sexuality. I fully agree with Augustine about one thing: our sexual energy is a powerful force that can eclipse the powers of our will. But unlike Augustine I don't believe our moral freedom has been forfeited. I do believe we are moral agents, and if we are to make wise choices we must first understand who we are. To do so heightens the possibility of our living lives that are rich in relationships and in love, lives that allow us to smell the flowers and even caress them without embarrassment. Amen.

The Reverend Arthur S. Vaeni is minister of the Starr King Unitarian Universalist Fellowship in Plymouth, New Hampshire. His essay is an edited version of a sermon preached to that congregation on October 26, 1997.

Readings on Sexuality and Spirituality

Susan Worst

The relationship between sexuality and spirituality encompasses many areas, from moral and ethical guidelines for sexual activity, to histories of religious attitudes toward sex and the body, to new understandings of sexuality as a sacred part of our being. Here is a short list of titles with which you may wish to begin to explore this rich topic.

UNDERSTANDING THE CURRENT CLIMATE

How did certain ideas about sexual behavior and gender roles come to be seen as "natural," or "the way things have always been"? Some of the most helpful books on sexuality and spirituality are devoted to this question, showing us how beliefs about sexuality arose in specific historical and religious contexts.

For example, *Adam, Eve, and the Serpent* (New York: Random House, 1988) is historian of religion Elaine Pagels's fascinating study of evolving attitudes toward sexuality in the first four centuries of Christianity. Pagels shows us that, while early Christians espoused a variety of views on sexuality, St. Augustine's equation of sexual desire and sin would leave the greatest mark on future generations.

Eros and the Jews: From Biblical Israel to Contemporary America by David Biale (New York: Basic Books, 1992) is an ambitious historical reconstruction of Jewish attitudes toward sexuality from the Bible onwards. Biale draws on a wide variety of sources—including religious writings, literature, folklore, and court documents—to portray what he describes as "a profoundly ambivalent culture."

Ethicist Kathy Rudy illuminates the sexual and gender values of the contemporary Christian Right in *Sex and the Church: Gender, Homosexuality, and the Transformation of Christian Ethics* (Boston: Beacon Press, 1997). Rudy helps us understand the Right's emphatic embrace of "family values," compulsory heterosexuality, and sexual purity, and argues that this vision springs from a theology that erroneously places family above community and God.

REREADING THE BIBLE

The Hebrew Bible and New Testament are often used to promote restrictive philosophies of sexuality, yet biblical study can also yield other interpretations. Several recent books have examined what the Bible has to say on the subject of sexual ethics, confronted the passages most troubling to contemporary progressive people of faith, and found support for more liberal views of sexuality.

In *Dirt, Greed, and Sex: Sexual Ethics in the New Testament and Their Implications for Today* (Philadelphia: Fortress Press, 1990), theologian L. William Countryman examines the teachings on sexuality in both the Hebrew Bible and the New Testament. The careful connections Countryman draws between the Bible's stories and laws and ancient beliefs about property and purity powerfully show how these ethical teachings do—and do not—apply to our own day.

Twice Blessed: On Being Lesbian or Gay and Jewish (Boston: Beacon Press, 1989), edited by Christie Balka and Andy Rose, contains two interesting essays that reexamine the Hebrew Bible. "In God's Image: Coming to Terms with Leviticus" by Rabbi Rebecca Alpert asks, "How do we live as Jews when the same text that tells us we were created in God's image also tells us that our sacred loving acts are punishable by death by decree of that same God?" The essay explores historical and contemporary views of the biblical verses that name sexual acts between men as an abomination. In the same volume, "In Search of Role Models" by Jody Hirsh locates same-sex-identified men and women in the Bible and Jewish history and explores the lessons that these figures have to teach us today.

The Sexuality of Jesus, by William E. Phipps (Cleveland: Pilgrim Press, 1996), cautions against the conventional view that Jesus was both single and celibate. Bringing together information about marriage practices of Jesus' time, analysis of New Testament sources, and readings from nonbiblical writings of the period, Phipps argues for a more open-minded understanding of both Jesus' own life and his teachings about women, sexuality, and marriage.

NEW THEOLOGIES, NEW ETHICS

Many recent Jewish and Christian writings have incorporated positive images of sexuality and the body into discussions of sexual ethics, of human wholeness, and of the relationship between humanity and the divine. Here are a few of these interesting and helpful works.

Carter Heyward's pathbreaking *Touching Our Strength: The Erotic as Power and the Love of God* (San Francisco: Harper and Row, 1989) puts forth a Christian sexual theology based on an understanding of the erotic as a force for justice and as an experience of God's love. Marvin M. Ellison's more recent work, *Erotic Justice: A Liberating Ethic of Sexuality* (Louisville, Ky.: Westminster/John Knox Press, 1996) asks the question, "What would a profeminist, gay-positive, and antiracist rereading of Christian tradition offer for the renewal of Christian sexual ethics?" It further proposes a sexual ethic that is sex-positive and anti-abuse and that "challenges traditional, fear-based moralities that focus on control of persons and their bodies."

In books such as *Embodiment: An Approach to Sexuality and Christian Theology* (Minneapolis: Augsburg, 1978); *Between Two Gardens: Reflections on Sexuality and Religious Experience* (Cleveland: Pilgrim Press, 1983); and *Body Theology* (Louisville, Ky.: Westminster/John Knox, 1992), theologian James B. Nelson has pioneered the effort to produce "a new level of consciousness about the ways in which our sexuality, for good and for ill, has shaped our expressions of faith." His books discuss the relationship between sex and love, sexual morality, marriage and fidelity, implications for the church, male spirituality, and many other topics.

Valuable for readers of any sexual orientation, the books of psychotherapist, priest, and former Jesuit John J. McNeill explore the integral relationship between sexual understanding, psychological health, and the spiritual journey. *The Church and the Homosexual* (Boston: Beacon Press, 1993); *Taking a Chance on God* (Boston: Beacon Press, 1988); and *Freedom, Glorious Freedom* (Boston: Beacon Press, 1995) also critique Catholic teachings about homosexuality, arguing that lesbians and gay men have important contributions to make to the church and its understanding of God.

In "Toward a New Theology of Sexuality," Jewish theologian Judith Plaskow proposes a Jewish feminist understanding of sexuality as "one dimension of our ability to live passionately in the world," and suggests how Judaism might accommodate this perspective. The essay appears in *Twice Blessed: On Being Lesbian or Gay and Jewish* (Boston: Beacon Press, 1989), edited by Christie Balka and Andy Rose.

Concise and accessible, *Love Does No Harm: Sexual Ethics for the Rest of Us* by Marie M. Fortune (New York: Continuum, 1995) puts forth a sexual ethic that, while based on religious principles, is meant to cut across religious lines. Fortune, an expert in sexual and domestic violence, founds her ethic on the principles of relational equality, consent, stewardship and safety, the sharing of pleasure, and faithfulness. The book includes a foreword by former US Surgeon General M. Jocelyn Elders.

EARTH-CENTERED AND NON-WESTERN TRADITIONS

Outside Christianity and Judaism, a rich variety of sexual and spiritual paradigms offer insight into contemporary dilemmas. Here is a small sampling of books on this complex and varied subject.

In *Dancing after the Whirlwind: Feminist Reflections on Sex, Denial, and Spiritual Transformation* (Boston: Beacon Press, 1997), L. J. Tessier explores the experiences of three groups of women whose sexuality is often repressed or denied: lesbians, survivors of childhood sexual abuse, and women with AIDS. Tessier holds up religious figures from around the world, including Buddhism, Hinduism, and Goddess spirituality, as models for the powerful benefits of sexual and spiritual wholeness.

The Red Thread: Buddhist Approaches to Sexuality by Bernard Faure (Princeton, NJ: Princeton University Press, 1998). This book, ranging over Buddhism's long history, describes both Buddhism's teachings about sexuality and the practice of its believers. Homosexuality and Buddhist monastic life are among the topics covered.

A classic work in Goddess spirituality, Starhawk's *Dreaming the Dark: Magic, Sex, and Politics* (Boston: Beacon Press, 1982, revised 1997) eloquently describes the power of erotic energy to transform and heal relationships, work, politics, society, and our attitudes toward ourselves and the world around us. *Cakes for the Queen of Heaven* by Shirley Ann Ranck (Chicago: Delphi Press, 1995), based on a popular adult curriculum of the same name, also uses images from Goddess spirituality to encourage women to understand and celebrate their sexuality as an integral part of who they are.

Susan Worst, an editor and writer, is the former religion editor of Beacon Press.

In Your Congregation

OVERVIEW

Comprehensive sexuality education programs offered by individual congregations can give people of all ages profound opportunities to deepen their faith. By helping congregation members explore how their religious values can affect their decision making, by promoting sexual and emotional health in our communities, and by fostering meaningful dialogue between peers, partners, families, and friends, such programs can prove invaluable.

With the support of clergy, religious educators, and lay leaders, this ministry can grow and flourish in your congregation. This section outlines concrete steps for effectively introducing a congregation-based sexuality education program. "Supporting Sexuality Education in Your Congregation" by the Reverend Cynthia Breen explains how to get things started and how to gain support, while "Handling Conflict Positively and Proactively" by Reverend Sarah Gibb Millspaugh offers suggestions for resolving disagreements that may arise over particular program offerings. "Distinguishing Debate from Dialogue" by the Public Conversations Project provides further guidance on making the process of introducing a sexuality education program an occasion for meaningful conversation rather than destructive argument.

Sexuality education is a ministry that can profoundly and positively move not just the participants in a program, but entire congregations. The stories of the First Congregational Church in Storrs, Connecticut; the First Unitarian Universalist Church of San Diego, California; and the United Methodist Church of Germantown, Pennsylvania, are included here so that their experience might help your congregation's ministry of sexuality education to reach its full potential.

Successful introduction of a sexuality education program in your congregation requires thoughtful preparation and deliberate work. Let this manual be your guide as you lay the groundwork for this meaningful ministry.

Supporting Sexuality Education in
Your Congregation

Rev. Cynthia Breen

Introducing sexuality education into your congregation can be a wonderful opportunity to put faith into action. It can provide a forum for members to talk about their sexual values and how these values can and do influence our society within the context of community. It can show members that sexuality education contributes to an objective held dear by virtually all people of faith: respect and justice for all, deserving of all. It can offer your congregation the opportunity to articulate and live these ideals, making it a richer source of life, hope, and support.

To offer sexuality education in a congregation is to acknowledge that human sexuality is simply too important, too beautiful, and too potentially dangerous to be ignored in a religious community. Sexuality education gives families and individuals of all ages the benefit of community support as they wrestle with sexuality issues and decisions. Although our society is saturated with images of sex, those images are often lacking in love and mutual respect. The education, worship, group activities, and advocacy encompassed in sexuality education can offer our children and youth a vision more consonant with our beliefs and values, and enhance intergenerational bonding and trust.

Yet, even in a congregation of like-minded people, sexuality education can be controversial. The subject is loaded with personal opinion and sometimes with fear and misunderstanding. Exploring sexuality education's programmatic possibilities requires hard work, courage, and an active commitment.

Effectively developing a congregational commitment, therefore, involves a four-part process of building allies, forming an oversight committee, educating and inspiring the congregation, and making the program an ongoing part of the congregation's ministry. If this work is not done, frustrations and misconceptions can develop, leading to controversy and division that can undermine or prevent the program's success.

BUILDING ALLIES

Building allies is the first step. Before attempting to institute a sexuality education program in your congregation, you will need the support of your congregation's ministers and lay leaders, such as the board of trustees, the religious education committee, the social action committee, and the youth committee. The support of individuals in the congregation who have a professional background in sexuality education or a related field, such as reproductive medicine or sex therapy, can also be valuable when representing the program to the congregation.

How can you gain this support? Learn about the history of sexuality education in your denomination and in your congregation, then explain your objectives for the program you'd like to offer. Give church leaders the opportunity to review the materials in the program, to meet with the curriculum teachers (if they have been selected), and to ask questions of the people most familiar with the program's content and values. If support doesn't come immediately, don't panic. Instead, work to continue the conversation, to discuss issues, to answer questions, and to meet individuals where they are. Expect to be an advocate for the sexuality education you believe in.

CREATING OVERSIGHT

Forming an oversight committee is the second step in building congregational support. Having committee members share the work of introducing and maintaining a program will not only make each person's workload lighter, but the input from various age and interest groups in the church will give many people a sense of ownership in the program. Their shared learning and wisdom will contribute to its success. Potential committee members include your congregation's director of religious education, parents, youth, professionals in fields related to sexuality, and representatives from other relevant groups within the church. In particular, seek to include members active in your congregation's social action committee; it is important that the religious education group is not alone in leading the effort to implement sexuality education.

What will the oversight committee do? Early on, this committee can help institute the program: creating a budget for program materials and teacher training, choosing the best resources and facilitators, coordinating sexuality education efforts with other congregational programming, and conducting activities to build support. The committee can work with the program's teachers to organize parent orientation sessions and obtain written permission from parents of all participants under the age of 18. Later, the committee can maintain the program, evaluate it regularly, and interpret the progress of the program to the congregation.

EDUCATING AND INSPIRING

The third step in developing a congregational commitment to sexuality education involves educating and inspiring parents, potential participants, and the congregation as a whole. Part of this effort might involve encouraging the congregation to think about religion and sexuality by leading worship services, sponsoring discussion groups, or developing reading lists on the subject. Survey your congregation about their interest in sexuality education and how sexuality relates to their theological and spiritual understandings. Explore whether your denomination has policy statements that an adult study group can read and discuss. Turn to your denomination's social justice department, religious education committee, or public policy office for resources that can support your efforts. The theological implications of sexuality, biblical references to sexuality, the responses of different world religions to sexuality, and issues of sexuality and justice can all be challenging and productive topics.

You will also need to educate the congregation about sexuality education and the specific curriculum you are using. Hold forums that are open to the congregation, or offer presentations about the program at congregational meetings. Announce the program in the congregation's newsletter and in Sunday bulletins. Display information on the religious education bulletin board and on the congregation's website. Provide more detailed handouts about the curriculum, the positive effects of comprehensive sexuality education, and the value of providing sexuality education in an environment centered on faith-based values. Consider joint programming for parents and youth, or courses especially for parents on communicating with their children about sexuality.

Your committee must not only educate, but also inspire. Sermons by the minister, by members of the congregation, or by youth can convey the importance and excitement that lies behind this effort. It is important to frame the issue of implementing comprehensive sexuality education in a broader context. When the congregation performs a child dedication or baptism, it commits to nurturing, loving, and educating that child. Sexuality education is part of that commitment we make to our families and our young people. It is part of the support we offer to families and children.

ONCE EDUCATION IS ESTABLISHED

The final step in starting a sexuality education program is institutionalizing it—making it part of the congregation's annual commitment to religious education. Institutionalization includes continuing administration of the curriculum by the oversight committee. The committee must also support the program teachers, by ensuring that they have proper training and by conducting background checks on new teachers. Finally, the committee should evaluate the program regularly, seek new or supplemental resources if needed, and ensure that the program continues to meet the congregation's needs effectively.

As sexuality education continues, so must advocacy. Each group of new parents, youth, teachers, and congregation members needs information about sexuality education and its connection to ministry. In addition, you may feel called to expand your congregation's advocacy into work across congregational or religious lines. Open up your sexuality education program to members of other congregations. Organize a workday at a center or local AIDS organization. Raise funds to benefit organizations that provide sexuality education. Collaborate with other organizations, religious or secular, to support comprehensive sexuality education in the community.

A major objective throughout this process is to increase communication between church members of all ages. Intergenerational communication is a valuable asset to any church. How rare are such opportunities in our society! By promoting sexuality education within your congregation, you can create opportunities to bridge these generational boundaries and to show that faith can shed light on the complicated issues of our times.

The Reverend Cynthia Breen is director of the department of religious education for the Unitaran Universalist Association and cochair of the Sexuality Education Task Force of the Unitarian Universalist Association and the United Church Board for Homeland Ministries.

Handling Conflict Positively and Proactively

Rev. Sarah Gibb Millspaugh

When introducing a sexuality education curriculum in a congregation, we do not have the power to prevent conflict. But we do have the power to decide how we will handle conflict when it arises. A positive, proactive response to conflict is essential to any sexuality education program's ultimate success. The following suggestions will help you in responding to conflicts when they arise.

1. Accept the inevitability of conflict by preparing for it. Individuals and groups *will* raise concerns, criticisms, and objections. Many can be quickly resolved with a discussion, but some cannot. Some concerns can be addressed with accurate information, other concerns are based on feelings, personal experience, and philosophy. Information alone will not address those concerns. It is often helpful for advocates and educators to decide how they will address particular concerns in advance.

2. Respond to criticism with care. If someone approaches you with a concern while you're scooping sorbet at the congregation's ice cream social, do not respond with a flip remark, even though it is not the right time or place to address the concern. Take the individual's concern seriously and invite him or her to speak with you about it further at an appropriate time.

3. Listen. Try to see things from the objector's perspective, even if you do not agree with his or her concern, objection, or criticism. He or she will appreciate being heard. Check with the objector to be sure you are hearing the concerns accurately.

4. Look for concerns behind the concern. Try to determine why the individual objects. Has he or she received accurate information? Does he or she have lingering unanswered questions about the program? Does he or she feel left out of the process? Does he or she object to all or part of the program? Why? Perhaps the objector holds deep philosophical differences with the program. An accurate understanding of the concern is necessary to respond effectively.

5. Correct inaccurate information and misconceptions with facts. Make sure that the concerned individual understands the program and its content. If his or her daughter returns from class saying, "Today we listened to awful rock songs about sex," the parent will be reassured to know that these are part of an activity that helps students critique media messages. He or she will be pleased at the opportunity to read that section of the curriculum. Parents are always entitled to review all curriculum materials used. Make sure the facts are clear. If the individual has misconceptions about sexuality education in general, use the resources in this manual to answer concerns about comprehensive sexuality education.

6. Recognize that sometimes objections are motivated by the objector's own unresolved sexuality issues. These motivations, whether conscious or unconscious, are often not publicly stated by the objector. In most cases it should be left to the objector to realize that he or she has unresolved issues. Saying, "I think you should go see a psychiatrist!" will only make the objector defensive and angry. Offering the objector an opportunity to participate in a sexuality education class, or recommending a good sexuality education book or video, is a better strategy if the objector seems open to it.

7. Don't try to change people's minds for them. Give people the space to be where they are. Present information to them, discuss issues with them, and let your views be known. Know that creating a space for a change in viewpoint is sometimes the greatest gift you can offer.

8. Recognize that your program can benefit from criticism. Be open to helpful suggestions, and be willing to adjust a program to accommodate valid concerns. Perhaps the parent orientation program really was incomplete. Perhaps the program's guest speaker really did say something that was developmentally inappropriate for the age group. On the other hand....

9. Do not accommodate every objector's concerns simply to preserve the peace. Don't remove the lesson plan on contraception because a small group of parents don't want it there. Consider excusing those parents' children from the lesson instead. Be flexible, but also be wary of compromising the program's integrity.

10. Use conflicts as opportunities for community education. Conflict can give program supporters an opportunity to share their positive experience with the program or articulate its connection to their religious values. Conflict can also identify aspects of the program that need clarification: perhaps the congregation didn't realize that each session opened and closed with a time of prayerful meditation, or that abstinence was discussed as well as safer sex.

11. Realize that conflict can open important conversations. Conflicts can serve as catalysts for conversations between friends, colleagues, classmates, partners, parents, and children. Through personal communication and sharing stories, individuals that were once opposed to a program can become its allies.

12. Understand that conflict can create community. A congregation that has struggled together is pulled closer when conflict is handled with intention. Discord can make a congregation appreciate their harmonious times together in a more profound way.

13. Accept that conflict is difficult. All of the positive suggestions and outcomes listed above do not diminish the fact that congregational conflict is challenging and often draining. Take care of your emotional, physical, and spiritual self and seek help from loved ones or caring professionals. Work to create spaces away from the conflict. Take the dog on more walks. Ride your bike. Meditate. Pray. Do not let your whole self be absorbed into conflict.

14. Always remember that participants in your sexuality education program are there voluntarily, with parental permission if they are minors. If substantial conflicts arise, suggesting that individuals leave the program is always an option. Participation in a sexuality education program should never be required.

15. Take the long view. In times of conflict, it's easy to forget that substantial and lasting change happens slowly. Remember that even if a program suffers setbacks in the short term, it will continue to move forward. Next year your congregation will start the program with more wisdom and experience than you did the year before. Each year will bring new opportunities for the program to improve, for congregational support to increase, and for sexuality education's promise to be realized.

Rev. Sarah Gibb Millspaugh served on the Sexuality Education Task Force, a joint committee of the United Church Board for Homeland Ministries and the Unitarian Universalist Association.

Distinguishing Debate from Dialogue

Public Conversations Project

This table contrasts debate as commonly seen on television with the kind of dialogue promoted by the Public Conversations Project.

Debate	Dialogue
Premeeting communication between sponsors and participants is minimal and largely irrelevant to what follows.	Premeeting contacts and preparation of participants are essential elements of the full process.
Participants tend to be leaders known for propounding a carefully crafted position. The personas displayed in the debate are usually already familiar to the public. The behavior of the participants tends to conform to stereotypes.	Those chosen to participate are not necessarily outspoken "leaders." Whoever they are, they speak as individuals whose own unique experiences differ in some respect from others on their "side." Their behavior is likely to vary in some degree and along some dimensions from stereotypic images others may hold of them.
The atmosphere is threatening; attacks and interruptions are expected by participants and are usually permitted by moderators.	The atmosphere is one of safety; facilitators propose, get agreement on, and enforce clear ground rules to enhance safety and promote respectful exchange.
Participants speak as representatives of groups.	Participants speak as individuals, from their own unique experience.
Participants speak to their own constituents and, perhaps, to the undecided middle.	Participants speak to each other.

Debate	Dialogue
Differences within "sides" are denied or minimized.	Differences among participants on the same "side" are revealed, as individual and personal foundations of beliefs and values are explored.
Participants express unswerving commitment to a point of view, approach, or idea.	Participants express uncertainties, as well as deeply held beliefs.
Participants listen in order to refute the other side's data and to expose faulty logic in their arguments. Questions are asked from a position of certainty. These questions are often rhetorical challenges or disguised statements.	Participants listen to understand and gain insight into the beliefs and concerns of the others. Questions are asked from a position of curiosity.
Statements are predictable and offer little new information.	New information surfaces.
Success requires simple impassioned statements.	Success requires exploration of the complexities of the issue being discussed.
Debates operate within the constraints of the dominant public discourse. (The discourse defines the problem and the options for resolution. It assumes that fundamental needs and values are already clearly understood.)	Participants are encouraged to question the dominant public discourse, that is, to express fundamental needs that may or may not be reflected in the discourse and to explore various options for problem definition and resolution. Participants may discover inadequacies in the usual language and concepts used in the public debate.

Reprinted with permission from the Public Conversations Project, 46 Kondazian Street, Watertown, Massachusetts 02472.

The Public Conversations Project, sponsored by the Family Institute of Cambridge, was founded in 1989 to apply the methods of family therapy to foster dialogue in the political arena.

First Congregational Church
Storrs, Connecticut

Rev. Sarah Gibb Millspaugh

Thoughtful preparation was the key to the successful introduction of a sexuality education program at the Storrs Congregational Church in Storrs, Connecticut, a United Church of Christ congregation.

Storrs Congregational was one of nine congregations to field-test "Created in God's Image," an adult sexuality education program published by the United Church Board for Homeland Ministries, in 1991. The ten-session program covers a broad range of topics, including male and female sexuality, sexual ethics, sexual violence, and public policy and advocacy.

Although the program itself began in January, preparations began months earlier. In September, three congregational leaders attended a three-day training session to learn about the program and how to lead it. In the following weeks, the three met with congregational staff and relevant groups within the church to discuss the possibility of implementing the program at Storrs. According to Duwayne Keller, one of the three organizers, "Discussions with all boards and committees that might impact the program, the church council, and pastors, director of Christian education, and other staff are a must. The cooperation and enthusiastic support of church leadership, both clergy and lay, are of utmost importance."

Once the support of congregational leadership had been secured, the program was introduced to the congregation as a whole during a worship service in October. Readings from "Created in God's Image" were included as part of the liturgy, and the sermon also discussed the importance of sexuality education for the church. One of the organizers also presented information about the program during the service, stressing that "the church is an appropriate and significant place to discuss issues and concerns related to human sexuality."

To underscore the usefulness of addressing issues of sexuality within the church community, Storrs Congregational's pastors led two additional programs in October and November. A five-week Bible interpretation class addressed human sexuality, and two Sunday-morning adult forums were also devoted to the topic. These sessions both signaled the pastors' support for the sexuality education program and helped generate enthusiasm and participants for it.

Finally, the program's organizers led two information sessions in November. "Informational meetings are extremely helpful," notes Keller. "The congregation should have the opportunity to meet the session leaders; understand the program's goals, methods, content; ask clarifying questions; and gain the feeling that they have been dealt with in an open and honest manner." Members of the congregation also had the opportunity to examine the curriculum, copies of which were made available in the church library.

After this extensive preparation, the program itself was a success, well-attended and positively evaluated. In addition to providing an informative experience for those who participated, it led to several other initiatives. A committee was formed to identify and plan future ministries to address issues of human sexuality. A pressing need for sexuality education for junior and high school students was identified, and programs for both youth and parents were conducted the following year. "Created in God's Image" was also repeated with different participants and session leaders. And in the mid-1990s, Storrs Congregational went through the Open and Affirming church process to become welcoming of gay, lesbian, bisexual, and/or transgender people.

A 1992 letter from the Human Sexuality Program Coordinating Committee, a group formed at the conclusion of the "Created in God's Image" program, outlined the rationale for this emphasis. "We believe that the church should be a place where we can talk about things that are very important, things that require us to make decisions, things that have everything to do with who we are and how we lead our lives." As the Storrs experience shows, with the proper preparation, such a hope can be realized.

CASE STUDY

First Unitarian Universalist Church
of San Diego
San Diego, California

Rev. Sarah Gibb Millspaugh

By encouraging conversation between youth and their parents, and by reaching out to other churches in the surrounding community, the First Unitarian Universalist Church of San Diego has made sexuality education, particularly for young people, a vibrant part of its ministry since the early 1970s. The church sees sexuality education as a reflection of its commitment to value all people, of "whatever tradition, gender, race, sexual orientation, or age." As director of religious education Liz Jones explains, "By honestly and openly addressing [our youth's] sexuality in appropriate ways we are honoring them as whole people. We acknowledge their worth and dignity. Through offering our sexuality program we not only honor each individual, but through knowledge we help each other along the path to respecting and honoring those who are different from ourselves."

Using a variety of programs over the years, including materials from Planned Parenthood and the Unitarian Universalist Association curricula *About Your Sexuality* and *About Sexual Abuse*, First Church offers the same course, concurrently, to both youth and their parents. Parents and youth learn about the same subjects and do the same activities at the same time as one another. The concurrent enrollment has succeeded in fostering communication between parents and their children. Conversations that begin in the car on the way back and forth to sessions have helped parents convey their values to their children and have allowed both parents and children to understand each other. Once parents establish their openness to talking about these matters, the stage is set for conversations to continue for years to come.

First Church's sexuality education program also reaches out to youth and parents from all eight of the Unitarian Universalist congregations in the San Diego area; leaders often come from these congregations as well. According to Liz Jones, this strategy not only helps to build community, but ensures the critical mass that sexuality education programs need to be effective. "One of the key components is encouraging in youth the ability to discuss these issues among themselves so they will have a comfort level to discuss with a partner their needs and concerns. If there are only two or three people, or if they are all male or all female, some of the value of the curriculum is lost. Appropriate space that offers some privacy is also important. We are able to offer that here."

Since the joint sexuality education program began, many other cooperative activities among area churches have emerged. Today, Unitarian Universalist churches in San Diego share an active and supportive ministers' group, a religious education network to share ideas and resources, a publicity committee that pools funds for advertising, and a leadership development team that provides workshops at area congregations.

Encouraging youth from many congregations to attend First Church's sexuality education program is not without drawbacks, Jones says. "When you have one large congregation with a large youth group and others with small or nonexistent groups, there is the potential of drawing the youth to the large group permanently. Some of our congregations have lost their youth to First Church's youth group. But we are sensitive to this, and we work hard to encourage the smaller congregations to send teams of kids and adults. If they come together they are likely to stay together in their home congregations.... We have had some congregations lose their youth, but we have also seen youth go back to their congregations inspired to create a strong youth program at home. It can work both ways."

How has the First Church's sexuality education program affected the congregation itself? For the individuals that participate, one of the most valuable results is the ability to talk comfortably and honestly about sexuality. An ability to respect and understand their peers fosters an ability to respect and understand their future partners. The opportunity to role-play asking a person out on a date, saying no to unwanted sexual advances, or convincing a partner to use a condom can prove very valuable when the situation arises later, in real life. According to Jones, the program has inspired some past participants to make life career decisions to work in community health outreach or nursing. It has inspired many more to make decisions about how to live their lives as healthy, loving people.

The sexuality education program has also made it easier for the congregation as a whole to comfortably address issues of sexuality. Each year, the congregation celebrates a "Wholly Family" worship service, which celebrates families of all kinds: families with single parents, stepparents, married/committed parents, same-sex couples, other-sex couples, absent parents, singles, widowed people, childless people, adoptive families, foster families, and more.

Furthermore, the congregation is a Welcoming Congregation with members of all sexual orientations and an active gay, lesbian, bisexual, and transgender group. This kind of acceptance and comfort level with people of all sexual orientations, Jones believes, is due in part to the adult participation in the sexuality education program. It has helped adults in the congregation work through their fears and stereotypes about gay, lesbian, bisexual, and/or transgender people, and to come to understand that sexual orientation and sexuality are part of being human.

CASE STUDY

First United Methodist Church
of Germantown
Germantown, Pennsylvania

Maggi Ruth P. Boyer and Ann Marie Donohue

TRAVELING NOTES: ONE CONGREGATION'S EXPERIENCE

The First United Methodist Church of Germantown initiated a collaborative effort with a professional sexuality education consultant in 1992 to develop a new way to provide sexuality education for the congregation. This program, guided by the authors of this article and working with the senior pastor and a committee of laypeople, demonstrates the usefulness of dialogue between two "cultures."

For background, the First United Methodist Church of Germantown is a metropolitan congregation with a membership of 1,000 and a worshipping congregation of approximately 250 on a typical Sunday. Many live within a four-mile radius, and many others come from other parts of the city, suburbs, and nearby New Jersey. The senior pastor, the Reverend Theodore Loder, has served the congregation since 1962.

During the past 35 years, the congregation has had a strong history of commitment to, and involvement in, social justice issues and the life of the surrounding and extended community. Such issues are addressed in the context of a perspective that views faith as relevant to all areas of life. This congregation has been among the first to hire an ordained woman as a staff member and to use inclusive language in worship services. It supports local efforts in housing, education, and medical care by participating in the Public Sanctuary movement of the 1980s, providing shelter and legal assistance to a Guatemalan family seeking political asylum, rehabilitating houses to sell at low cost, joining with other churches to provide shelter and support for homeless families, and working for social justice in Central America, Haiti, and South Africa.

This history of involvement in social justice is an important element of the congregation's culture. It reflects a willingness to confront challenging and controversial issues and to explore these issues in the context of religious faith. How a congregation has dealt with difficult or controversial issues in the past gives valuable clues to its resources, processes, and strategies that might also apply to the issue of sexuality.

In this congregation, for instance, involvement in social justice issues has fostered the development of a culture where dialogue is important, where all issues are part of the life of faith, where justice is an expression of love, and where there is an underlying commitment to the concept that "we can all take risks together."

In addition, the congregation has a strong commitment to the centrality of worship as the heart of its life, and to the importance of small groups for ongoing learning, mutual support, and personal growth.

When selecting a faith community with which to work, sexuality educators may find that whether the community has discussed sexuality in the past may be less important than whether it has developed a culture of dealing with controversial and challenging issues in constructive ways.

FROM HISTORY AND CULTURE TO SEXUALITY EDUCATION

The church began a two-year process of study and discussion in 1988 to decide whether to become a Reconciling Congregation, a grassroots movement in the United Methodist Church through which a congregation affirms inclusion of gay and lesbian persons in the life of the church, including ordained ministry.

It subsequently voted in 1990 to become such a congregation. The decision was a continuing expression of the congregation's concern with issues of justice. It was also consistent with a faith stance that included a willingness to address controversial or difficult issues.

During this time, it became apparent that it was not only sexual orientations that were difficult to discuss, but sexuality itself. People in faith communities can be uncertain about sexuality. They may struggle with aligning their values and behavior. They may celebrate and rejoice in the wonder of sexuality. People in faith communities reflect the secular culture in which they live, and they are not all of one mind, even within the same congregation.

Following its decision in 1990, the church's Administrative Board established a Committee on Religion and Sexuality whose mission was, and continues to be, to expand the focus of opportunities for continued study, discussion, and growing understanding of sexuality in the light of faith. This was accomplished through programs for young people as well as adults, with a focus on faith and values, ethics and relationships, and on understanding what it means to be fully faithful as well as a fully sexual person.

It was significant that the Reverend Loder took a clear stand on the importance of addressing these issues. From the pulpit he spoke about sexuality as part of the mystery, the struggle, and the gift of being human, which gave the congregation a framework for further discussion.

As the Committee on Religion and Sexuality continued its work, the members decided that the issues were too vast and too specific. They also realized that they needed to learn how to create a context for addressing issues that are normally considered private and that most people are unaccustomed to discussing. They, therefore, sought the help of a professional sexuality educator.

At the recommendation of another pastor, the committee decided to invite a private consultant, who was also the director of training and education for Planned Parenthood of Bucks County, to work with them. The members had a preconceived image of a sexuality educator as someone who would emphasize facts at the expense of the deeper issues of identity, relationships, and values. They were surprised to find that the professional sexuality educator had worked with other congregations as well as clergy on the same issues and that she had demonstrated a sensitivity to faith contexts and issues.

All committee members and the Reverend Loder attended an initial consultation session with the sexuality educator to make certain that all issues, fears, and concerns were addressed and to make certain that any course of action was congruent with the new life and theology of the congregation.

A NEW DIRECTION/MODEL

Out of this lively session, an exciting decision emerged: to train committee and church members to become Sexuality Resource Persons for the whole congregation. These individuals would plan and lead discussions and programs in faith and sexuality and would have informal conversations with church members.

This decision was seen as an excellent alternative to having an "expert" drop by and conduct discussion sessions or work with the youth of the church. Such training would strengthen the confidence and skills of Resource Persons. Realistic limits could be identified and understood concerning what help Resource Persons could and could not provide. Training would also help them to clarify their own values and goals and to build trust with one another.

If the Sexuality Resource Persons were going to be accepted as facilitators of discussions about faith and sexuality, it was important that they reflect the diversity of the congregation and that they include known and trusted individuals. An effort was made to invite participation by people of different ages, races, sexual orientations, family status, and ethnicity.

Since the committee had as part of its mandate to provide programs for the church's young people, it sought the involvement of the church staff member who worked with youth as well as a teacher in the church's junior high school-age group. All who accepted the invitation to the training understood that participation was preparation for more active leadership in programs of faith and sexuality. Fourteen people accepted this invitation.

Two full-day training sessions were conducted for the Sexuality Resource Persons in 1992. The first day focused on an exploration of sexual development and issues throughout the life cycle, an examination of personally held values and beliefs, and personal growth and development. Information was presented on topics such as adolescent sexuality, sexual orientations, pregnancy prevention, sexually transmitted infections, talking about sexuality, barriers to effective communication about sexuality, male and female puberty experiences, and male and female gender issues. Teaching methodologies included small group work, male and female "fishbowls," crayon drawings, anonymous questions, and values voting.

The second day focused on the role of the Sexuality Resource Person, including identifying agencies and organizations appropriate for referrals, understanding appropriate limits of confidentiality, learning active listening skills, finding answers to difficult questions, identifying bibliographic resources, and developing strategies to support each other.

Participants reported that the training provided a uniquely helpful opportunity to discuss, question, and reflect on sexuality in a safe and supporting climate. They pointed to a sense of mutual respect and comfort when evaluating the training experience.

WHAT HAPPENED NEXT?

While the group felt their training was helpful, they were still concerned about leading discussions on sexually sensitive issues with others. Two additional steps proved helpful and instrumental.

First, a discussion session was scheduled for the parents of teens. While the consultant helped design and facilitate this meeting, much of the leadership was provided by the Sexuality Resource Persons. This practice, with the assistance of a trusted "expert," helped these individuals bridge the gap between training participant and group facilitator.

Second, a session with the consultant was scheduled several months after the training sessions to allow the Sexuality Resource Persons to talk about issues, concerns, questions, and problems that had come up. Such meetings have continued once a year. In addition, the consultant has made herself available to the Sexuality Resource Persons and the committee by phone and in person when necessary or requested.

Finally, and perhaps most uniquely, the formation of the Sexuality Resource Persons group was affirmed in the church's worship service. Shortly after the training, a Sunday service was dedicated to the theme of "Faith and Sexuality" and members of the Resource Group offered their reflections as part of the sermon. The names of all the Sexuality Resource Persons were listed in the church bulletin, thus affirming the importance of the effort and inviting the congregation to participate in a continuing conversation about faith and sexuality.

LESSONS LEARNED

In the five years during which the Sexuality Resource Persons have provided leadership, they have become instrumental in developing and implementing learning opportunities about faith and sexuality. They have:

- led discussions on "Faith and Sexuality" for young people in the fifth through twelfth grades
- led discussions on "Sexuality and the Bible" and "Sexuality Over the Lifespan" for adults
- designed and facilitated special congregational events, usually held in the evening, on "Faith, Sexuality, and Singleness" and "Faith and Sexuality in Films" (using such films as *The Priest* and *The Last Temptation of Christ*). Pastoral staff facilitated these discussions
- implemented an event, "Why Is Sexuality So Hard to Talk About?" by using guided imagery and small work groups
- conducted small work groups to discuss reading from the book *Embodiment*.

Those involved in the sexuality education program also learned some lessons from mistakes. As a result of problems they have:

- incorporated the Committee on Sexuality with the Sexuality Resource Group (Individuals involved with both groups had complained about too many meetings.)
- developed plans to immediately utilize the skills of newly trained Sexuality Resource Persons (Many newly trained individuals dropped out of the program when they weren't immediately called upon to participate.)

- developed a method to gather data about the relationship between affirming Sexuality Resource Persons by the congregation and the growth of requests for information (Such data was not originally collected.)
- formed working groups of Sexuality Resource Persons interested in creating and implementing individual programs/series (All individuals originally worked together to develop all programs.)

The success of these programs has not eliminated the congregation's desire to have presenters or facilitators from outside the church. Such programs provide well-attended adjuncts to the ongoing work of the Sexuality Resource Persons, help to identify other areas of interest, and integrate the experience into the ongoing life of the sexuality program of the congregation.

THE JOURNEY NEVER ENDS

The congregation's decision to actively explore issues of sexuality in the light of their faith both reflects and affects the life of the congregation. The presence of a Committee on Religion and Sexuality, of Sexuality Resource Persons, and of strong pastoral support for this effort work together to continually "lift up" issues of faith and sexuality as important and appropriate concerns for the church.

This is perhaps the single most significant aspect of this work, for the exchange between the two "cultures" or "worlds" of sexuality education and congregational life is not a final destination, but an ongoing cycle of planning, exploring, learning, reflecting, resting—and then beginning all over again by determining the next phase of the journey.

Excerpted with permission from "The Journey of Sexuality Educators to Faith Communities" by Maggi Ruth P. Boyer and Ann Marie Donohue from SIECUS Report, Vol. 26, No. 1, October/November 1997, copyright © 1997 by the Sexuality Information and Education Council of the United States, 130 West 42nd Street, Suite 350, New York, New York 10036-7802.

Maggi Ruth P. Boyer, MEd, is national training director of Advanta Information Services in Springhouse, Pennsylvania. Ann Marie Donohue, PhD, is a staff associate at the First United Methodist Church of Germantown in Philadelphia, Pennsylvania.

In Your Community

OVERVIEW

Advocating for comprehensive sexuality education in community settings such as public schools is both similar to and different from advocating within one's religious community. In secular and religious communities alike, ignorance and fear often present the strongest opposition. Our society is deeply uncomfortable with sexuality in general. Because the vast majority of North Americans have not participated in formal, comprehensive sexuality education at any time during their lives, many adults naturally will have misconceptions about what a comprehensive sexuality education program might include. These concerns can be dispelled with facts about specific programs and about sexuality education in general. Part I of this book contains several articles that can help.

Yet community organizing presents distinct challenges as well. The first is learning how to work as a person of faith in a secular setting. The first two articles in this section, "Navigating the Political Landscape: A Roadmap for People of Faith" by Sandy Sorensen and "Using Religious Voices to Confront the Religious Right" by Rabbi Lynne Landsberg *et al.*, explain the contributions that people of faith can make to the political process, as well as how religious individuals and organizations can practice activism without violating the separation of church and state.

A second difference between congregational and community activism is that the community stage is likely to be much larger, requiring a more skillful presentation of the message and a wide variety of techniques for communicating that message to diverse audiences. Controversies in the public sphere play out in the boardroom, the newsroom, the classroom, and the courtroom. They are picked up by the media and transmitted via print or picture to living rooms everywhere. They affect what goes into the ballot box and what comes out of the mouths of elected representatives. In public controversies, image is important. It is essential to appear more reasonable than those who oppose you. Do not try to convert your opponents to your way of thinking. Instead, present your arguments to the undecided. Be proactive in promoting your message; don't let your opponents define your message for you.

The next six articles in this section address these challenges. "Public Speaking Tips about Homophobia for People of Faith" by the Reverend Meg Riley illustrates the technique of reasonable argument and also provides useful ways for handling antigay rhetoric that may arise in discussions of sexuality education. "The Role of Coalition Building in Community Education and Advocacy" and "Education and Media Campaigns" by Advocates for Youth, "Pitching Reporters" by the SPIN Project, "Working with School Boards to Ensure Comprehensive Sexuality Education" by SIECUS, and "Lobbying: The

Art of Persuasion" by Advocates for Youth offer useful techniques for educating other community organizations, politicians, the media, and the public effectively.

A final difference between congregational and community advocacy is that one is much more likely to encounter organized opposition. Focus on the Family, Concerned Women for America, and Citizens for Excellence in Education are among the many national organizations with roots in conservative religion and religious right politics that have opposed comprehensive sexuality education. (Many such groups support abstinence-only curricula, discussed in "The Case for Comprehensive Sexuality Education" at the beginning of this book, which teach children that sexual abstinence is the only correct sexual choice for unmarried people.) Very vocal, very organized local groups may arise as well. Opposition from the religious right plays a role in the two case studies at the end of this section: the story of Zion United Church of Christ, which brought a Planned Parenthood health center to Henderson, Kentucky, and of the citizens of Hemet, California, who halted the use of an abstinence-only curriculum in their schools.

For additional information about national opposition to comprehensive sexuality education, consult "Resources for More Information" in the Appendix. Your local Planned Parenthood chapter can also tell you about antisexuality education activity in your area.

Navigating the Political Landscape:
A Roadmap for People of Faith

Sandy Sorensen

Having embraced the call to public policy advocacy and social justice witness, how do we proceed? The following markers can help us along the way:

Hold fast to the vision: A common concern—and rightfully so—among people of faith seeking to work in the political sphere is discerning when advocacy violates the traditional separation of church and state. The distinction is an important one. It is illegal and inappropriate for religious organizations to engage in partisan or candidate-focused advocacy. A religious organization can engage in political work without being partisan. Religious organizations can legally and effectively engage in issue- and belief-based advocacy.

As people of faith, we bring the gift and the responsibility of holding true to a vision of right relationship in human community that transcends any singular party, ideology, or platform. Separation of church and state is not a barrier to the participation of faith advocates; rather, it reminds us of our vital role as ongoing, critical partners in the larger public dialogue. As such we may support the exercise of government power when it is just and contributes to the common good. Similarly, we must hold governments accountable when power is exercised unjustly; when power causes suffering for human beings and for creation

Speak your truth and hear the truth of others: The most powerful tool we have as advocates in the political sphere is our stories. It is our stories and the realities they reveal that have the power to persuade, to change hearts and minds. When we speak out of the particularity of our own stories and beliefs, we are more likely to stay grounded in the truth while not denying the truth of others.

It is important to remember that we know a piece of the truth. But we also must remember that it is only a piece of the larger whole. In speaking from your own experience and conviction, you may encounter points of disagreement with other faith perspectives and even with the perspectives of others in your own denomination. Yet it is possible to respectfully claim the faith grounding for your position while acknowledging that all may not be of one mind on a particular issue.

Speaking from one's denominational identity is different from speaking on behalf of the denomination. Progressive people of faith have been particularly reluctant to claim their faith identity and grounding in their political work, for fear of imposing religious views on others. We can responsibly and respectfully articulate our own faith perspective without denying others the right to do so.

Continue to educate yourself and your community: As faith advocates, it is no less important for us to understand the facts behind the issues. We are much more likely to be heard by others if we have done our homework. While it is important for us to clearly articulate the faith basis of our position, we must also be clear about what is at stake and what needs to change.

Be mindful of your fallibility: To be faithful, responsible, and effective advocates, we must acknowledge that our judgments, discernment, and positions may not represent an objective truth. We must hold ourselves accountable by continually engaging in self-reflection, by returning to God's vision of human community when our plans, strategies, and visions fall short. They will inevitably fall short. Our ability to move forward rests on our willingness to see things differently, to hear new voices, to ask new questions.

It is important to identify and help shape forums for honest, respectful dialogue, where we may be touched by new realities and more dimensions of truth.

We are called to take a stand: Recalling that politics refers to the way we order our common life, we are, inescapably, political beings as well as social beings. If we do not take a stand on a particular issue, we ultimately give our approval to the prevailing position or policy approach, even in our silence. It is not possible to remain politically neutral, for in drawing back from the political sphere we implicitly support things as they are. It is important for us to know that we are called to choose where we will stand, and to do so wisely and responsibly. Bishop Desmond Tutu reminds us that neutrality is a false choice, saying, "If an elephant is standing on the tail of a mouse and you remain neutral, the mouse will not appreciate your neutrality."

Tap the power of your faith to transform political debate: Even as we remember our limitations in the political sphere, it is equally important to consider the invaluable strengths we bring to our political work. In a "zero sum game" world, where one can win only if others lose, our faith enables us to raise a different possibility for our common life. As people of faith we are about more than simply change—ultimately, we are about transformation.

We do not simply seek greater access to power, but we seek to transform the nature of power itself to serve the common good. During a panel of "Women and Global Governance" at the Fourth United Nations Conference on Women, one panelist remarked that it is "not enough to get into a room you have long been denied access to, only to find the furniture doesn't fit you." Faith allows us to envision a room comfortable enough for all. As people of faith, we are able to enter the political sphere, not settling for the "lowest common denominator," but seeking the "highest level of cooperation."

Know the value of the religious community's leadership: If we do our homework and advocate responsibly, not only will our voice as religious advocates be heard, it will be sought and welcomed. Clearly articulated without being stated in absolutes, the faith basis for our position on an issue is often seen as a refreshing change from the grounding of narrow self-interest. Legislators and their staff members express great appreciation for the capacity of the religious community to rise above competing interests to give witness to a larger good.

Sandy Sorensen is the associate for resource development at the United Church of Christ's Office of Church and Society.

Using Religious Voices to Confront the Religious Right

Rabbi Lynne Landsberg, Rabbi Daniel Swartz, and Aaron Bisno

Any successful campaign to confront the agenda of the religious right will need the involvement of at least some segments of the local religious community. This chapter briefly outlines why such involvement is critical and discusses how to organize most effectively within the religious community.

WHY INVOLVE THE RELIGIOUS COMMUNITY?

1.   *The power of a religious response to religious claims:* The religious right often claims to have God on their side or at least to represent the religious perspective. They accuse their opponents of being hostile to religion. The simplest and most effective way to reveal the falsehood of such claims is to have in your coalition active representatives of religious communities who oppose the agenda of the religious right from a religious viewpoint. Representatives of such viewpoints clearly illustrate that your side also has moral and value-based arguments it can marshall. Inclusion of such individuals or faith groups indicates clearly that religious people believe the separation of church and state to be good for religion, that religious people support gay and lesbian rights, and that religious people—in fact, most mainstream religious denominations—support a woman's right to choose for reasons rooted in their faith. With religious support for your cause, you will have come one giant step closer to defeating the religious right.

2.   *The resources of the religious community:* Religious communities are ready-made, "pre-organized" communities with a variety of resources, including: organized human-power, fully equipped buildings, public relations connections, and financial resources that potentially can be put to your use. It should be noted, however, that churches, synagogues, mosques, and other religious organizations are primarily religious, not political bodies; people do not join their particular religious institution in order to support political activity. Nonetheless, with this caveat, you will find religious institutions that will gladly join you in your endeavor and may very well make their resources available to you.

3.   *If you don't, the religious right will:* The religious right uses religious organizations as its primary organizing focus. You can be assured that if you do not reach out to the religious community in your area, the religious right will. In particular, the religious right is making a concerted effort to win the support of minority churches. Unless you present yourself and your cause effectively to these churches, they may be persuaded to ally themselves with the religious right. Conversely, if these churches ally themselves with you, it will immediately broaden the impact of your efforts.

58

HOW TO ORGANIZE WITHIN THE RELIGIOUS COMMUNITY

1. *Work within existing institutional infrastructures:* Before approaching individual churches, synagogues, mosques, etc., you should tap into already existing interfaith networks and denominational institutions. Most communities have some sort (or several sorts) of interfaith clergy councils. In small towns, these are volunteer-run groups, while in larger cities they may have professional staff. In addition, areas with significant Jewish populations usually will have a board of rabbis with representatives from all the different movements within Judaism. Finally, most denominations have some sort of regional structure, such as a diocese or presbytery. By working through these types of structures, you will be able to reach larger numbers of religious leaders and congregations with less effort. Ask for permission to use a mailing list or to have an article included in a regional newsletter. See if you can speak at a meeting to many members of the clergy at once. Ask one sympathetic staff member at the regional level to give you names of clergypersons who also are likely to be sympathetic to your cause.

2. *Clergy are the key to their congregations:* Once you have utilized regional structures to the fullest extent possible, you can turn to individual congregations. To get a particular church, synagogue, etc., on board your campaign, you will first need approval from the clergyperson in charge. As you try to get such approval, keep two points in mind. First, clergy respond best to other clergy. Once you have one minister, rabbi, priest, etc., who strongly supports you, ask him or her to help you with calls to other members of the clergy. Second, members of the clergy are usually overworked. Make your presentation brief. Show how he or she can plug into your campaign with a minimal time commitment. Have written material available for the clergyperson to include in a sermon or use in a congregational newsletter. Ask for names of lay leaders in the congregation who you can turn to for more extensive commitments.

3. *Don't forget potential allies in noncongregational institutions:* The Jewish community in particular has a variety of nonreligious Jewish institutions that may be effective allies, ranging from community relations councils to local chapters of national groups such as the American Jewish Congress and the American Jewish Committee. The Protestant and Catholic communities also take part in private, voluntary organizations and/or ecumenical, lay movements such as the YWCA, the YMCA, and Churchwomen United. Such voluntary organizations and lay movements should be sought out. Additionally, do not overlook state or local chapters of interreligious, political networks such as Interfaith Impact for Peace and Justice and the Religious Coalition for Reproductive Choice.

4. *Choose your allies carefully:* Not all religious institutions are alike; they differ greatly both between and within denominations in terms of political influence and attitudes. You will need to make decisions, such as: do I first approach congregations that are likely to be sympathetic, or do I focus instead on those with the greatest numbers and political resources? Once you have some members of clergy on board, you can ask them for their evaluation of how likely it is that a particular congregation might join with you and what resources they might bring to your campaign.

5.   *Indicate how the religious institution might benefit:* Know how your campaign can benefit your allies even as they help your cause. First of all, many members of the clergy see themselves as being called to work for justice, but they may not know exactly how to do such work. By giving them a good cause and an effective organization to work with, you are giving them a desirable opportunity. Second, their congregation may receive positive recognition through your campaign, making its members feel more excited about their participation in the congregation as a whole and perhaps even attracting new members. Finally, your organization may help with leadership development within the congregation.

6.   *Know how to respond to church/state and tax-exempt concerns:* Some members of the clergy or congregational leaders may hesitate to get involved in your activities because they are concerned about violating the separation between church and state. You should make it clear to them that speaking out on issues is not a violation of the law interpreting the constitutional separation of church and state, and that such efforts do not jeopardize their tax-exempt status. The law states that a congregation cannot spend a "substantial" portion of its budget on direct lobbying (visiting congresspeople, letter writing, bulletin articles urging action on specific legislation, etc.). Because the term "substantial" is ambiguous, the rule of thumb is that no more than five percent of a congregation's budget may be used for such activities. It is highly unlikely that a congregation would come close to using five percent of its budget for such purposes, because most of the lobbying and/or letter writing is done by individual members and not the institution itself. Furthermore, there is no cap on the amount of money, time, or resources a congregation and/or clergyperson may use to speak out on issues, generally through articles, op-eds, sermons, public speeches, educational forums, etc., so long as they do not address specific pieces of legislation.

Note well, however, that congregations may not get involved in partisan support for candidates and/or political parties without jeopardizing their tax-exempt status, but they can get involved in such nonpartisan activities as sponsoring a voter registration drive or a multicandidate debate.

7.   *Know what to ask for and of whom to ask it:* Even though members of the clergy are often overly busy, they do respond positively to invitations to speak at public rallies, press conferences, etc., and they can be powerful speakers. Ask the clergy for opportunities to publicize your cause within their congregation, either through a congregational newsletter or through an opportunity to speak at the congregation. Ask them as well to put you in contact, not only with other members of the clergy, but also with the lay leadership of the congregation most likely to assist you. These lay leaders may be able to help with publicity, space for meetings, letters and phone calls to elected officials, and large turnouts for public gatherings.

8.   *Build long-term relationships:* For the involvement of the religious community to be most effective, you have to develop long-term relationships and not merely approach religious leaders for crisis intervention. This can be done structurally by inviting religious leaders onto any formal board structures you develop. Equally important as such formal recognition, however, is involving the religious community in the early planning and strategy stages of your campaign; such involvement gives them ownership of the issue.

Furthermore, once involved in the planning, they will be able to help you shape your campaign to use the resources of the religious community most effectively.

(The authors owe a debt of gratitude to Kim Bobo of the Midwest Academy for inspiration for sections of this article. For more in-depth information on organizing the religious community, we refer you to "Working with Religious Organizations," pp. 140ff. in *Organizing for Social Change: A Manual for Activists in the 1990's*, published in 1996 by Seven Locks Press, Santa Ana, Calif.)

Rabbi Lynne Landsberg, Rabbi Daniel Swartz, and Aaron Bisno wrote this article for the Religious Action Center (RAC) of Reform Judaism. The RAC is the Washington office of the Union of American Hebrew Congregation and the Central Conference of American Rabbis.

Public Speaking Tips about Homophobia
for People of Faith

Rev. Meg Riley

DON'T respond defensively to homophobic scriptural citations by engaging in a boxing match style of dialogue about them. Example: *"God made Adam and Eve, not Adam and Steve!"* "That's ridiculous! The creation story is a myth to explain human creation—scientific research shows that the first human was a woman in Africa!"

> DO use humor and keep a light touch. Examples: *"God made Adam and Eve, not Adam and Steve!"* "Are you saying that heterosexuals are responsible for the fall of humankind then? I'll try not to be bitter." Or *"Gay people don't have to act on their sexual desires. God can heal them."* "But, as I read Scripture, 'just say no' didn't even work in the Garden of Eden!"

DON'T fight with an idiot. Someone watching the two of you won't know which one of you is the idiot. Example: *"Gay people should all be killed."* "It's people like you who should be put in jail! You're a danger to democratic society!"

> DO appeal to the moderate observers. *"Gay people should all be killed."* "I know that the majority of Americans are as frightened by your words as I am. Every poll shows that we support fair, nonviolent treatment for all people."

DON'T let someone else frame the debate or set the parameters of the discussion. *"Our founding fathers intended this to be a Christian nation, and the Bible clearly condemns homosexuality!"* "This is not a Christian nation, and never has been. Why, Thomas Jefferson explicitly said that ...."

> DO speak positively and stay on track. *"Our founding fathers intended this to be a Christian nation, and the Bible clearly condemns homosexuality."* "The people who founded our great nation bequeathed us with a Constitution and Bill of Rights which clearly promote freedom of religion. These documents provide the basis for our covenant for living together in peace. That's why we're concerned that our community is being divided by antigay violence and fear."

DON'T demonize or insult anyone. *"I just don't think gay people should have special rights."* "Only a bigot or a homophobe would say that!"

DO differentiate leaders from followers; use language of reconciliation and compassion. *"I just don't think gay people should have special rights!"* "I am concerned that Americans, who strongly oppose discrimination, are being misled about exactly what this initiative means. Equality is not a special right."

DON'T allow homophobes to monopolize religious language. *"God's word is good enough for me: to be gay is an abomination."* "Regardless of what you read in the Bible, this is not a Christian country and the Bible should not govern our laws."

DO claim the moral high ground; cite Scripture; use your own religious language. *"God's word is good enough for me: to be gay is an abomination."* "Jesus never mentions homosexuality at all, but he does say to love your neighbor as you love yourself, and that's how I try to live." or "The God that I know is a God of love, who does not see any person as an abomination."

DON'T allow the debate to be framed as religious people vs. secular gays: *"Religious people are concerned that militant gays will destroy our families."* "We're here, we're queer, get over it!"

DO speak openly about your own faith as it informs your commitment to gay, lesbian, bisexual, and transgender issues. *"Religious people are concerned that militant gays will destroy our families."* "In my congregation, we're concerned about the high incidence of gay-bashing in our town. We feel that we best embody God's radical commitment to love by teaching our youth that violence and intolerance are neither moral nor acceptable."

DON'T get sidetracked into discussions of whether people choose to be homosexual or what percentage of the population are gay. *"Homosexuals could choose to change if they wanted to."* "You're either born gay or you're not! Why, studies show that ...."

DO stay focused on your own talking points. *"Homosexuals could choose to change if they wanted to."* "Americans deserve equal treatment under the law. People could choose to change religions or marital status, but that would not make discrimination against them acceptable. While we still don't know much about the cause of sexual orientation, Americans do know that antigay discrimination is wrong."

DON'T globalize the issue or use frightening rhetoric. "This is the first step towards death camps! First they came for the Communists, and I did not speak up because I was not a Communist!, etc., etc." You may believe it, but to the average person you sound like a nut.

DO speak specifically about how homophobia affects your community in tangible, measurable ways. "What would this initiative mean? It would mean that I could be legally fired from my job because I am gay and I would have no channels for correcting that injustice!"

DON'T try to terrorize people into voting on your side. "We are in pre-Nazi Germany, and you have the chance to vote against Adolph Hitler!"

DO lift up a vision of unity. "In hard times like these, we all need each other. Candidates like X divide us from one another and waste our precious resources."

The Reverend Meg Riley is the director of the Unitarian Universalist Association Washington Office for Faith in Action.

The Role of Coalition Building in Community Education and Advocacy

Advocates for Youth

Coalition building and public education play vital roles in implementing policies and programs for adolescent reproductive and sexual health. Coalitions provide a structure for allied groups to pursue a unified goal, coordinate strategies, and pool resources. Broad-based coalitions demonstrate wide support for particular policies or programs.

Coalitions can serve the purpose of educating policymakers and the public regarding adolescent and reproductive health services. Coalition members act to lobby policymakers, write letters to the editor, speak with the press, attend community meetings, and give public testimony. By so doing, policymakers and the public are afforded accurate and compelling information regarding adolescent health and are therefore more likely to demonstrate support for related policies and programs. Coalitions act to mobilize this support, demonstrating to policymakers that constituents care about improving or maintaining adolescent access to sexuality education and health services. Coalitions also provide a powerful counterpoint to organized opposition.

Organizations and Groups to Involve

- young people
- teachers' unions
- social service agencies
- family planning providers
- youth-serving agencies
- racial/ethnic associations
- civil rights groups
- civic groups
- elected officials
- child abuse and neglect groups
- AIDS prevention and service organizations
- school faculty/staff, including health educators and nurses
- public and community health professionals and officials
- adolescent pregnancy prevention organizations
- religious leaders and organizations
- LGBTQ advocacy groups
- local chapters of national advocacy organizations
- school-based and school-linked health center staff

The following are some basic tips for creating and maintaining a coalition. Activities through which the coalition can promote adolescent reproductive and sexual health programs and policies are also included.

There are four steps to increasing community involvement and building support for adolescent reproductive and sexual health programs:

- Work in coalition
- Conduct research
- Prepare materials
- Conduct educational campaign.

The following explains each step in greater depth.

STEP 1: Work in Coalition

Coalitions are invaluable because they bring people and resources together from all sectors of the community and provide visible signs of community support. Working in a group helps increase quality as well as the quantity of work, and prevents burnout by spreading responsibilities. Coalitions allow individuals and groups to contribute their unique expertise, as well as to educate and mobilize their particular constituents. Coalitions can help identify genuine concerns and engage in group problem-solving. Once a program is implemented, coalition members are ideal for providing services and resources for program operations.

Coalitions are hard work, however. Keep in mind the following pitfalls and work to minimize the usual problems found in coalitions:

- Coalition members' interests may conflict.
- Building consensus is a time-consuming process.
- Logistics become more complicated.

Guidelines for Effective Coalitions

Develop a statement of purpose and goals. The "statement of purpose" can be broadly worded to reflect the philosophy of the coalition and permit a wide range of groups to participate. "Goals" should be specific, achievable, and measurable. An organization's membership in the coalition symbolizes their commitment to the goals, and is indicated by endorsement of the coalition's statement of purpose.

The statement of purpose should be broad, but not so broad that groups who would actively impede the overall purpose are eligible to be members. For example, if the coalition seeks comprehensive sexuality education, a group that opposed any discussion of abortion would not be an appropriate member. The coalition could work with nonmember groups on other projects, but without jeopardizing the strategic work of the coalition.

The statement of purpose is also a place to clarify that your program is comprehensive and to address obvious criticisms. Highlight program components such as "involving parents" and "promoting abstinence" to forestall criticism and prevent misunderstandings. For example, a coalition seeking comprehensive sexuality education might adopt a statement of purpose that the coalition seeks sexuality education which includes information about abstinence and the full range of family planning options, as well as builds skills to communicate with parents and peers about sexuality.

Establish a structure and leadership roles. Coalitions are most effective when all members have a voice and know they will be heard. Creating maximum involvement does not negate, however, the need for organized leadership and structure.

Select leaders. Choose chairs and clearly define their responsibilities. It often helps to have cochairs whose skills complement each other and who represent organizations willing to commit significant time and/or resources to coalition efforts. Roles can be shared or rotated.

Create a broader leadership team that includes representatives of the major interest groups. A diverse team will be more successful in providing effective leadership on an issue as complex and multifaceted as teen reproductive and sexual health.

Select spokespeople who will represent the coalition to the media. These should be people with experience in interacting with the media, who are comfortable in that role. The spokespeople may or may not be the same people as the leadership team, but this may simplify communication. One of your spokespeople should be an articulate teenager. Agree on a process for handling media requests and opportunities.

Share responsibilities for the work through task forces or committees. These allow more people to become invested in the group, and can either be permanent or just for a specific project. Define responsibilities and the decisions that can be made without the broader coalition.

Create and follow a realistic timeline. Rome wasn't built in a day. A realistic and strategically developed timeline is one of the most important tools for a coalition. Some of the most successful programs take over a year to be implemented. A realistic timeline with targeted activities every month will help ensure the coalition remains focused and realistic in expectations. Short-term activities could include bringing 10-15 new organizations into the coalition; a medium-term goal could be the introduction of legislation supporting your program; a long-term goal is the passage of that legislation.

Establish a coalition identity. A coalition is more than the sum of its parts. To establish identity and generate excitement for the goals, members need to see how they fit in. Letterhead stationery listing coalition members and an updated membership list fosters ownership and the respect of those who receive coalition communications.

Be explicit about how decisions will be made. Coalitions often make decisions by consensus. This doesn't mean that everyone has to agree on everything. Rather, a majority agrees and no one feels so strongly opposed that they would veto or publicly oppose the effort. Decide what will happen if consensus cannot be reached. Decide which decisions will be made by the leadership team and which are so important or sensitive that the entire membership needs to be involved. Determine in advance what issues must come before the entire coalition and how the coalition will make decisions quickly.

Hold regular meetings. Meetings should be held frequently enough to respond to current situations, and can be scheduled weekly, bimonthly, or monthly. Hold meetings at a convenient time and location; start and end on time. Consider whether meeting times should rotate between day and evening hours and between locations.

Keep people informed. Maintain up-to-date mailing, email, phone, and fax lists of coalition members and key contact persons. Keeping members informed maintains trust, interest, and involvement. It also minimizes misunderstandings and identifies points of disagreement before they become problems. Coalition members should receive minutes from meetings, updates, press articles, and information on future events. Advance notice of meetings and other events encourages participation in important discussions and decisions.

Expand your base. The number and range of groups coalitions attract reflect their success. The public and politicians will judge the strength of the cause by the coalition list, both who is involved and who is missing. Teens are clearly the group most affected by the issue, yet they are often left out of the advocacy and planning process. Other groups to approach are listed in the chart.

Ensure that these groups are aware of the problem the coalition seeks to address and that they understand the need for action. Make clear how they will benefit from being part of the coalition effort. Give them an easy way to join the coalition and support your program as part of the solution. Outreach through members' organizational resources (newsletters, meetings, staff) to educate and enlist more support for your coalition goals. As each new group joins, add them to the coalition stationery and list of supporters.

Involve youth. Articulate and committed young people help the coalition remain true to its mission. Moreover, youth are excellent spokespeople for programs designed to address their needs. Young people can also organize students and other young people to support the program. Many community groups already work closely with youth and should be targeted for involvement with the coalition. Teens know their peer opinions and needs better than most adults; be open to young people's suggestions and seek their input. Involve youth in meaningful ways and encourage them to represent the coalition to the media.

Develop materials. Create 1-2 page materials describing the problem you are concerned about and the proposed program's ability to address it. Compile a larger packet of materials that can be distributed to the community and to the media. See Step 3 (below) for more information on what types of information to create.

Develop educational campaigns. In order to win support for your program, you must be ready to advocate on its behalf. Survey the policymakers who will be involved in approving, funding, and implementing your program, and start educating them. Start with firm supporters and move on to moderates and undecideds. Coalition members can testify at hearings, organize letter-writing campaigns, write letters to the editor, etc. Refer to the Lobbying ["Lobbying: The Art of Persuasion"] and Media ["Education and Media Campaigns"] handouts in the last section of this manual as well as the Public Education Campaign section [Step 4] below.

Monitor planning and implementation of the program. Once legislation has been passed, the expertise of coalition members can be useful in design and implementation. Members may be asked to sit on the design team or advisory committee, provide education in classrooms, train program staff, develop written or visual materials, or accept referrals for other services.

STEP 2: Conduct Research

Poll after poll shows that most Americans support adolescent reproductive and sexual health programs. Those who are not initially supportive usually need more information to convince them to be proponents. They may just need to understand why the program is important and what its components are in order to become supporters, or they may have specific questions or concerns that can easily be answered. Others need to feel that representatives from their community have been involved in developing the program in order to become its champions.

Three types of research are necessary in order to answer these questions and maximize public support.

Prepare a needs assessment. The coalition cannot build support for a program unless it can make a compelling case for why this program or policy is needed, and what its effect will be. This analysis is typically called a "needs assessment." Research the situation in your community and make comparisons with national rates. What has changed over time?

Assess the current political situation. The coalition cannot work effectively for change without understanding the political environment and the players. Who does the coalition need as a supporter of the program, and what is their background and viewpoint? What policymaking body will make this decision, and what is its structure for doing so? Who is running in upcoming elections, and how will their success affect program implementation?

Know the opposition. Strategic planning for program success must include an understanding of what opposition the program will face, and from where this opposition will come. Research the most likely concerns and criticisms to be raised and prepare in advance to respond with current research and facts.

It is vitally important to anticipate organized opposition from extremist conservatives. Programs designed to address sexual and reproductive health are a flash point for extremist groups, and may generate vocal and sustained criticism. The extremists effectively publicize misinformation about adolescent reproductive health which must be corrected if the public is going to support programs under attack.

Research any extremist group affiliates in your community and collect their materials on the issue at hand. Find out which decision makers are associated with these groups and what their arguments are likely to be when approached about proposed programs.

STEP 3: Prepare Materials

Advocacy is easier if the coalition has gathered or created information persuasive to groups being approached for support. Materials may be created for specific audiences whose concerns vary, since parents, the press, legislators, business people, and teens will be interested in and concerned by different aspects of the problem at hand and the coalition's suggested solutions. Leave materials behind whenever coalition members visit policymakers or other interested groups.

Educational pieces should be short, easy to read, and to the point. They should explain the need for the program as well as describe the program's components and its intended effects. Educational materials are an appropriate place to respond to questions, concerns, and misinformation about the program. (See the Media section for more information on press-related materials and the Needs Assessment for useful data.)

Materials to create:

- Information about the coalition: list of members, statement of purpose and goals.
- National, state, and local statistics on adolescent reproductive and sexual health connected to the proposed program or policy, such as rates of sexual activity, lack of access to medical care, rates of pregnancy, reported AIDS and STD cases.
- Factual information that describes the local situation, explains why the proposed program of policy is necessary and describes its intended effects.
- Information on similar programs implemented elsewhere.
- Research and other facts that rebut expected criticisms from the opposition.
- Supportive media coverage of the issue such as a newspaper clipping or editorial.

STEP 4: Plan and Conduct an Education Campaign

A successful strategy for program implementation must include education targeting three distinct groups that, while distinct, influence one another: policymakers, the public, and the media. Without public support, policymakers will be reluctant to back potentially controversial programs. Media coverage educates the public about the need for and structure of the proposal. An educated public is more likely to press for political support of the program. Without political support, the program cannot succeed, particularly when legislative approval is required. Specific educational activities are listed later in this section.

Ensure that factual information presented in clear and accessible language reaches the public BEFORE misinformation about a proposed program does. Communicate about why the program is needed, what the program goals are, how teens will benefit from it, and how the public can observe and participate in the program. Never let a communication void be filled by misleading, inaccurate information; instead, reach out with information before there is a crisis of communication and public trust.

The best way to educate is to USE THE MEDIA. People who oppose adolescent reproductive and sexual health programs use the media, and program proponents must also. Use the media and other forums to challenge misrepresentation and ask for clarification. Never allow misinformation about a proposed program to stand unchallenged.

The next section of this manual ["Education and Media Campaigns"] gives tips on working with the press to promote a program, but several points bear repeating. Use the media to respond to concerns about the program, particularly those originating in press arenas such as letters to the editor or op-ed columns. Write articles for the local paper and promote coalition members for interviews on television and talk radio. Use press releases and news advisories to keep the media informed about the state of teen health in your community, and how the coalition goals will help improve the situation.

An educational campaign involves targeted advocacy. "Lobbying: The Art of Persuasion" gives specific tips but, in general, the coalition should plan to visit everyone involved in promoting, approving, and implementing the program. Meet first with the most supportive individuals or agencies and ask them to join the coalition. Their name on the coalition membership will invite others to join.

Coalition members should go directly to influential and supportive community members and groups, describe the program and why it is needed, and ask them to publicize the coalition's goals. Providing materials for organizational newsletters and meetings is an easy way to provide information to a broad group of people. Speaking at meetings and other group activities is another effective way to get out the word on the coalition's program.

OTHER ACTIVITIES FOR EDUCATING THE PUBLIC

All of these events present opportunities to reach the public with detailed information about the proposed program. The following opportunities can be used to answer questions, respond to concerns or questions, and encourage broader participation in the group working to promote the program.

- Give a presentation at board or membership meetings of civic, professional, and/or advocacy groups and ask them to endorse the coalition's goals.
- Create and distribute materials targeted for a specific audience, such as parents; these materials can include questions and answers, reports, fact sheets, etc.
- Hold or participate in community forums or briefings for parent groups, parent-teacher associations, neighborhood associations, etc.
- Testify at meetings of policymaking bodies such as school boards, city councils, legislatures.
- Organize coalition members' constituencies to engage in a letter-writing campaign to policymakers and/or the papers.
- Conduct a petition drive among the general population or among specific groups such as students; then hold a press conference and present these petitions to policymakers.
- Conduct polls or surveys to gauge and/or illustrate community support.
- Write articles about the program for organizational newsletters.

- Hold speak-outs, protests, or rallies to illustrate support for the program.
- Write letters to school boards, the Department of Education, and other government agencies concerned with the issue.

Reprinted with permission from Advocating for Adolescent Reproductive and Sexual Health: The Advocacy Kit, *copyright © 1996 by Advocates for Youth, 1025 Vermont Avenue, NW, Suite 200, Washington, DC 20005.*

Advocates for Youth (formerly the Center for Population Options), based in Washington, DC, is dedicated to creating programs and promoting policies that help young people make informed and responsible decisions about their sexual and reproductive health.

Education and Media Campaigns

Advocates for Youth

Media coverage is important because it carries your message to a much larger number of people than can be reached independently. Carefully planned media strategies help identify supporters, answer people's concerns, and persuade those who are undecided. The media also can diffuse criticism by providing a forum to explain a program and demonstrate thoughtfulness, sensitivity, and candor.

Luckily, adolescent sexuality is a story that will attract press attention. Unluckily, it is also a story too-often covered irresponsibly or without a great amount of depth. Given our society's discomfort with adolescent sexuality, media coverage of the issue often fails to explore the complicated and inter-related aspects of teen health and the prevention programs designed to improve adolescent futures.

Successful media plans usually follow a four-step process:

1. Define the role of the media in outreach efforts. Be aware of media coverage of related issues (sexuality, HIV, adolescence) and provide copies of past coverage in briefing packets. Keep records on local and national press (both those who have been contacted and potential contacts). Keep accurate mailing, telephone, and fax lists of the press in your area.

2. Determine what press activities to hold and which materials to have on hand as background or current information. Consider sending out press releases, creating a press packet, holding a press conference, or using a variety of other techniques.

3. Be aware of the leading spokespeople for the opposition and the media strategies they employ; be prepared to respond.

4. Evaluate your press campaign. Keep track of stories, determining how the story was presented, who was quoted, and what kind of follow-up may be necessary.

THE SPOKESPERSON AND INTERVIEWS

The Spokesperson: Press calls should be routed to a designated spokesperson (or spokespeople) to establish a regular contact for the reporter and to allow for follow-up. This person should be articulate and well-versed on adolescent health and pregnancy prevention issues. They should be able to speak clearly and directly to the issue without using jargon or terms unfamiliar to the audience. If the respondent is not a spokesperson for the organization, but is providing background information, make the relationship clear and let the reporter know who to talk to for attribution.

When You Don't Know: If the spokesperson does not know the answer to a question, it is important to say so. Reporters have the right to ask anything and expect that the spokesperson will answer to the best of his or her knowledge. The respondent has the right not to be drawn into issues that are inappropriate for comment. ANY remarks made to the media are liable to be used. If you don't want something published, don't say it. If there is a subject on which you don't want to be quoted, the safest rule is to not talk about it. Do not be drawn into criticism of colleagues or other organizations. Reserve criticism for real adversaries or for motivating public officials.

The Story: It is crucial that the spokesperson plan in advance what points to make and how to make them succinctly. Anticipate difficult questions and practice answering them in a role-play situation before interviews. Focus on two to three points and stress these points in your conversation or interview. Short snappy sentences (15-20 words) that stand alone are "sound bites"; make it easy for the media to use your words by providing them in this format. Use a technique called "bridging" to ensure that your points are made. For example, if the interviewer asks an irrelevant question, say "I think the real issue [or question] is ...."

THE PRESS INFORMATION PACKET

One of the most important items for a media campaign is the press information packet. It contains basic background material on the program's issues and describes the coalition. It can be used to insert press releases and advisories for conferences or briefings. A standard packet includes:

- Information about the coalition: a list of members, statement of purpose, and goals;
- Contact information for the press spokesperson, including a phone number;
- Background (such as fact sheets) on adolescents and AIDS, STDs, sexual activity, and pregnancy/birth/abortion rates;
- Information on similar prevention programs across the country;
- Favorable press coverage of the coalition or similar prevention programs;
- Information on how the proposed program can address a need in the community;
- Materials for a press conference, such as news advisories, news releases, statements from the coalition leadership, copies of their speeches or testimony.

WHEN THE PRESS CALLS

Calls should be directed to a spokesperson who will either respond to the inquiry or refer the reporter to an appropriate person for additional information or an interview.

Respond to all media calls. Don't avoid press calls. Leaving a "no comment" impression may arouse suspicion. Responding quickly will increase the chances of being quoted and cited in the final story. Practice making your 1-2 points before calling the reporter back.

Be aware of "sensationalist" journalists, those who have stated their opposition to your program, or those who work for newspapers with an editorial position against it.

Be especially cautious when working with these journalists. Think about how to work with these journalists before they call; you may decide not to give interviews to these organizations.

WHEN CONTACTING THE MEDIA

Develop a press list including contact information for the various departments you will be contacting (PSA, events listing, health writer). Your press list should contain the television, radio, and newspaper outlets in your area, including university papers, community newspapers and radio stations, regional magazines, and military press officers.

Learn the deadlines for media outlets on your press list and research the demographics of their target or primary audience (e.g., teenagers, sports fans, affluent). To be most effective in dealing with the press, also research the contact for your calls and materials. The following are some suggestions:

- Newspapers and Magazines: Contact the assignment editor or the assignment desk.
- Television: Start with the assignment desk. TV public service directors and editorial directors are also good contacts, particularly for public affairs programming. Some correspondents also take part in deciding which stories are covered.
- Radio: Identify news directors and talk show producers to whom the interview may be suggested. Shows whose primary audience is teens are a particularly good place to call for coverage.

EVALUATING PRESS RELATIONS

Keep copies of press coverage that mentions your efforts, as well as records of press materials and media contact information. The crucial factor in understanding and evaluating press experience is in setting realistic expectations.

A news story should present the proponents' side of the story fairly and evenly and present other viewpoints. It should incorporate at least one of the major points raised in the interview. It will quote spokespeople accurately. But most important, a press piece should not only educate the community about challenges the program confronts, but also lay the foundation for greater awareness and support.

MEDIA ACTIVITIES

News Releases. A news release is a one- to two-page (500-800 words) description of an event, program, or activity. It can stand alone or be enclosed with additional materials and resources. News releases should be distributed with sufficient lead time and include the following: one or two quotes from spokespeople; date on which the information can be released; facts: who, what, where, when, why, and how; contact name and telephone number. Make your point in the first few paragraphs. Distribute a news release by mail, fax, messenger, or at conferences and press briefings.

News Advisories. A news advisory is sent to announce an event or specific news; it is a simple one-page document that invites coverage of an event. Include a description of what is happening, when, why, where, and who is participating. Fax the advisory to your contacts 1-2 days prior to the event.

News Briefings and Press Conferences. Briefings should be reserved for announcements that cannot be communicated well in a press release. When possible, schedule the briefing to last up to half an hour between 12-2 p.m. Use a location convenient to the reporters such as a press club or downtown site. Have press kits available at the event, and post someone from the coalition at the door. A briefing on the overall issues of the program is appropriate at the beginning or after a great deal of change.

Public Service Announcements (PSAs). PSAs are a good way to publicize events. For radio, write a 15- to 20-second statement or announcement and submit it by fax or mail to the PSA contact. Television PSAs will need to be produced, but your only cost is for production, not distribution. Many newspapers will print information from PSAs in their community calendars and announcements sections.

Local Cable Access Programming. Cable access channels offer access to equipment, air time, and consulting and are an excellent venue for local issues. PSAs, panel discussions, and other programming are possible; contact the local cable company for more information. In many areas, cable channels will film public forums or debates.

Buying Space or Time. Buy space for a prepared advertisement to appear in local newspapers or magazines. Newspapers and magazines have rate cards that explain ad sizes and prices. Buying time for radio advertisements is relatively inexpensive. Check with local stations for rates, listenership, and technical requirements for submitting advertisements. Some stations allow radio personalities to read ad copy on the air; others use only advertisements that are produced on tape.

Letters to the Editor. Newspapers frequently print letters to the editor that address an issue which has been in the news recently. The letters to the editor section is one of the most read sections of the paper, and an ideal place to respond to criticism or concerns. Letters should be persuasive, brief, and use statistics from reputable sources. A prominent member of the community could be asked to write a letter or sign a letter drafted by another coalition member.

Guest Editorials. Guest editorials, or "op-eds," are brief opinion pieces or essays on topics in the news. Op-eds should be approximately 500-800 words in length and make one major point, backed up by reputable statistics and compelling stories. As with letters, a prominent member of the community could be asked to write an editorial or sign one drafted by another coalition member.

Letters to Media Professionals. Maintain press contacts through letters to reporters, editors, talk show producers, and editorial boards. Use letters to suggest interviews or topics for press consideration, to acknowledge good coverage of an issue, or to praise a reporter or editor.

Appearing on TV or Radio. TV and radio stations often look for community members to comment on current events. You and the coalition can call or send information suggesting yourself/the spokesperson as an appropriate guest for a specific show. Once you are invited onto a show, research the other guests' views. To make the case more compelling, use stories to illustrate your points in addition to facts. Speak in short, crisp sentences. It's harder to provide background in these mediums than in print, so assume no prior audience knowledge when you make your case. On TV, wear bright solid colors, and avoid wearing glasses.

Reprinted with permission from Advocating for Adolescent Reproductive and Sexual Health: The Advocacy Kit, *copyright © 1996 by Advocates for Youth, 1025 Vermont Avenue, NW, Suite 200, Washington, DC 20005.*

Pitching Reporters

Strategic Progressive Information Network Project

Pitching your event to reporters is imperative for getting good coverage. Don't just fax and mail them the media advisory; call them and pitch the news!

TIPS FOR THE PITCH

- Don't call the press simply to ask them if they received your media advisory. Reporters get too many press releases every day to let groups know they've arrived. Pitch them the story and reference the media advisory.
- Don't waste reporters' time. Pitch stories when you actually have news. Pitch them in person or pick up the phone and call them.
- You will have only a few minutes during the initial pitch call.
- You must get their attention and capture their interest immediately.
- Reporters do not have time for long-winded pitch calls.
- Have a good "hook" for a story and "frame" the news so it has greater significance, drama, controversy, timeliness, and impact for more readers, viewers, and listeners. The better you frame your news the greater your chances of scoring a media hit (see example below). Communicate your key messages to the reporter during the pitch.
- Be timely, not obnoxious. Don't call reporters when you know they are on deadline (for example, late afternoon for morning paper reporters). They'll probably hang up on you out of irritation or try to get you off the phone immediately, if you get them at all. Mid-morning is a good time to pitch. Also, be sensitive to their mood. If you sense they are rushed, offer to call back later or at least acknowledge their predicament ("Listen, I know you're very busy, but do you have a moment or should I call back later?").
- Be friendly, enthusiastic, and helpful. If you are not excited about the story, the reporter probably won't be either. But don't go overboard in your enthusiasm. Give reporters the necessary information, offer to provide more, then get off the phone.
- Try to target specific reporters with whom you have relationships.
- If they have done a piece on the issue or a similar subject, reference their prior work. At least target reporters in the relevant section of the paper. Does your news pertain to the "Metro," "Lifestyle," front page, or some other section? If you must make a "cold call," ask the general assignment editor or producer who you should talk to. Then call that reporter.
- Don't pitch more than one reporter at a news outlet in the hopes at least someone will cover you. If you do talk to more than one reporter, let the other reporter know you've talked to someone else.

- Make certain your pitch contains the who, what, where, when, and why.
- Emphasize the visuals, especially for television.
- If you get voice mail, leave the basic information and then call back.
- If the reporter you call is not interested or on another beat, ask who else you can speak to.
- Close the deal. Ask the reporter if he or she is coming to the event or is interested. Most will not immediately commit over the phone, but will think about it.

THE PHONE PITCH—AN EXAMPLE

CBE: Hi, this is Wendall Chin from Communities for a Better Environment [your name and group here] calling. I know you're very busy, but I wanted to take just a moment to tell you about an exciting [controversial, huge, dramatic... pick an adjective!] event happening next week regarding El Niño [your date and hook here].

REPORTER: Yeah, what is it? I can't talk long....

CBE: We faxed over a media advisory this morning for our upcoming protest in front of the San Francisco sewage director's office. We are conducting a protest to expose the inadequacies of the new $1 billion sewage system. You've written a story about how beaches up and down the California coast are being closed because of polluted runoff caused by the storms. Well, the same thing is threatened here but even bigger. The storms are exposing the problems with the inferior sewage plan and that may have dire and controversial consequences long after El Niño leaves. Our new sewage system is already failing Mother Nature's test. It must be overhauled.

REPORTER: That sounds interesting. Tell me more.

CBE: We are presenting thousands of postcards signed by concerned residents of San Francisco to the chief of sewage and we are demanding an urgent meeting with him. The polluted runoff not only is threatening to close tourist beaches, but it affects in particular low-income people who fish the Bay and the beach for their livelihood. Everyone suffers because of the problem. The protest will be Wednesday, Feb. 25, at 12:30 p.m. in front of the sewage office at 1155 Market Street near 7th St.

REPORTER: Do you have background on this problem?

CBE: Yes, we've got facts on the closings of the beach and a fact sheet on the sewage plan, which we think is seriously deficient. El Niño is a huge problem that has implications way beyond the stories of homes falling into the sea. The sewage system has cracks that we have been trying to fix for years. It's hurting the community by allowing sewage to overflow onto the beaches and into the Bay. Thousands of families are outraged, and El Niño is making it worse.

REPORTER: What's going to happen at the protest?

CBE: We will present the postcards signed by outraged families. There will be exciting visuals of storm umbrellas stenciled with messages, dirty sand and brown suds from the closed beaches, and protesters in "hazardous material" uniforms with beach balls and fishing poles. Does this sound like something you would cover? [If not, ask who else you should speak with.]

REPORTER: Uh, maybe.... I'll check with my editor.

CBE: Great. We hope you can cover it. Let me know if you need more information. Thank you.

Reprinted with permission from the Strategic Progressive Information Network (SPIN) Project of the Independent Media Institute, 77 Federal Street, San Francisco, California 94107.

The SPIN (Strategic Progressive Information Network) Project, created in 1997, provides media technical assistance to nonprofit public interest organizations around the nation. It is housed at the Independent Media Institute, formerly known as the Institute for Alternative Journalism.

Working with School Boards to Ensure Comprehensive Sexuality Education

Sexuality Information and Education Council of the United States

In most communities, local school boards have the final say over the sexuality education curriculum used in the district. School board members may not be familiar with issues related to sexuality education and may view debate over this topic as a contest between special interest groups. They may be invested in voting a certain way because of the manner in which the debate over sexuality education has been framed in the press or by people who have contacted them.

The most important fact to consider when trying to convince school board members to support a comprehensive approach is that these people serve in an elected office and require the support of the community to continue in their position. If you are able to mobilize broad and widespread support for comprehensive sexuality education, you are much more likely to ensure that such programs are implemented or preserved.

The following tips can help you influence your school board.

Organize school board candidate forums.

Organize these forums well before the election. Prepare questions for the candidates that include their positions on sexuality and HIV/AIDS education. You may also want to ask questions related to outcome-based education, voucher initiatives, moments of silence, and self-esteem courses. Publicize candidates' responses widely.

Meet with school board members.

Invite one other person to join you when you meet with each school board member. Use these meetings to gain an understanding of board members' views on education. Are they concerned about test scores? Pregnancy prevention? Getting back to the "three R's"? Try to emphasize common ground in these meetings. If you are a parent with children in the district, be sure to let school board members know.

Provide tailored information to school board members.

Send follow-up information responding to each school board member's individual concerns.

For example, if you need to convince a "back to basics" school board member about the importance of sexuality education, provide him or her with information about how sexual health problems can get in the way of academic achievement. If a board member is concerned about the budget, let him or her know about the cost of implementing a fear-based sexuality education program. Emphasize that these programs are expensive and that funds have already been spent to secure the current program, which is supported by parents, students, and teachers.

Attend school board meetings.

These meetings are often sparsely attended; make sure someone attends each one. Showing up before a controversy occurs will give you more credibility with the school board.

Encourage community members to contact school board members.

Even a few calls or letters can make a big difference in the outcome of sexuality education debates on the local level.

Testify before the school board.

You can support comprehensive sexuality education by speaking on this issue before your school board. Coordinate testimony with other people who support comprehensive sexuality education to ensure that the most effective messages are being provided to the board throughout the meeting.

Be respectful toward the board and toward community members who oppose comprehensive sexuality education. The strongest arguments are reasonable, but include some emotional appeal and passion. When possible, also share your perspective as a parent or grandparent rather than only as a professional.

Use consistent, well-thought out messages.

Work with other individuals in your community group to develop three or four key messages in support of comprehensive sexuality education in your community. These messages should be concise and convincing. Make sure that supporters repeat these messages in school board meetings and other public forums.

Identify candidates to run for school board seats.

Help ensure that supporters of comprehensive sexuality education are elected to the school board. Consider running yourself. Remember that although you may not be able to do this as part of your job, you can always assist on your own time.

VOTE!

School board elections attract low voter turnout. You can make a big difference in the kind of sexuality education provided in your community by reminding friends and colleagues to vote.

Reprinted with permission from The SIECUS Community Action Kit: Information to Support Comprehensive Sexuality Education, *copyright © 1997 by the Sexuality Information and Education Council of the United States, 130 West 42nd Street, Suite 350, New York, New York 10036-7802.*

Lobbying: The Art of Persuasion

Advocates for Youth

People use the voting booth to let their elected officials know how well they're doing. But there are other opportunities to communicate with decision makers, and many different methods for doing so, such as visiting, calling, or writing legislators or presenting testimony.

Advocacy can occur at any time. Particularly in local policy bodies (such as school board or city council), many opportunities exist for sharing opinions. Advocacy can occur when you encounter a legislator in the hallway or the post office. You can sign up to speak at a public hearing or write to legislators about your viewpoint. There are also specific points in the legislative process when bills are most readily affected. The state legislative research office, League of Women Voters, or the Secretary of State's office can provide information on the legislative process in your state. Use this material to help decide upon the most effective strategy for making your views known to decision makers.

It is also useful to understand parliamentary procedure, which is an operating system used by legislators. Parliamentary procedure is complicated, but well worth understanding. Little-known rules and procedures are often used to defeat or weaken proposals without generating public notice or allowing legislators much opportunity for negotiation. Likewise, rules and procedures can be used to advance legislation and bring it to a vote. Familiarity with the parliamentary procedure used by the targeted political body will increase advocates' ability to strategize for success under many scenarios.

GENERAL TIPS FOR ADVOCACY

Target your efforts. Survey the policymakers who will be involved in approving, funding, and implementing your program, and decide who you will approach, and in what order. Start with firm supporters and move on to those who are moderately progressive or undecided in their views. You may want to begin with legislators on the committee that will first hear the bill and members of a friendly caucus, such as the Women's Caucus. Be certain your own legislator knows your position on the bill.

Be gracious. Always begin by thanking the legislator for providing the opportunity to hear your ideas, opinions, etc. Legislators who support adolescent reproductive and sexual health, in particular, receive a lot of negative attention from the opposition. A sincere "thank you" will be greatly appreciated.

Be professional. Be professional in both dress and manner; don't say negative things about other legislators or public figures.

Be focused. Stick with one issue per call or letter. Information about more than one topic will only confuse the message and dilute your point.

Do your homework. As part of your preparation, research the legislator's position on your issue. You can find out through voting records, speeches, newspaper articles, debates, and other organizations that work on this area. Advocacy organizations, particularly those with Political Action Committees, often track legislators' votes and can provide voting guides. Explore the legislator's personal connections with the issue: do they have teenagers themselves? Frame your presentation for maximum effectiveness based on your knowledge about the legislator's constituency, views, background, interests. Different arguments are compelling for different people; use the most persuasive argument for this person. It might help to role-play what you want to say at the meeting, and practice responses to possible comments.

Make a personal connection. No matter how insignificant you may feel it is, if you have friends, relatives, and/or colleagues in common, *let the legislator know!* In particular, let the legislator know if you are a constituent. The legislative process can be very informal and, although a personal connection makes no difference in your presentation, it may make the difference in your effectiveness.

Consider yourself an information source. Legislators have limited time, staff, and interest in any one issue. They can't be as informed as they'd like on all the issues—or on the ones that concern you. *YOU* can fill in the information gap. Encourage the policymaker to ask questions about the program or issue.

Tell the truth. There is no faster way to lose your credibility than to give false or misleading information to a legislator.

Know who else is on your side. It is helpful for a legislator to know what other groups, individuals, state agencies, and/or legislators are working with you on an issue. Providing this information also illustrates that your group represents many more voters. Bring coalition members and young people with you on lobbying efforts. It is also important to keep in touch with your allies so that advocacy efforts are coordinated and relevant information is shared.

Know the opposition. Anticipate who the opposition will be, both organizations and individuals. Tell the legislator what opposition arguments are likely to be and provide clarifications and rebuttals. The ability to anticipate criticism and defend your position will make a difference.

Don't be afraid to admit you don't know something. If legislators want information you don't have, or ask something you don't know, tell them. Then offer to get the information they are looking for and *DO IT!*

Be specific in what you ask for. If you want a vote, information, answers to a question, signature on a petition—whatever it is—make sure you ask directly and get an answer.

Follow up. It is very important to find out if the legislator did what she or he promised. Send a thank-you letter after your conversation, restating your position. It is also very important that you thank the legislator for a supportive vote, or ask for an explanation of an unsupportive vote.

Stay informed. Legislation changes status quickly and often. Amendments or other committee actions can radically change the effect of a bill without receiving much publicity. The sponsor or legislature's research office can help identify where in the process the bill is currently located, and what its current language is.

Don't burn bridges. It is easy to get emotional over issues you feel strongly about. That's fine, but be sure that you leave your relationship with the legislator on good enough terms that you can return to them on that or another issue. Don't get into a heated argument with a legislator, and never threaten them. Your strongest opponent on one issue may be a great proponent on another!

Remember, you're the boss. Your tax dollars pay legislators' salaries, pay for the paper they write on and the phones they use. YOU are the employer and they are the employees. Be courteous, but don't be intimidated. They are responsible to you and, nine times out of ten, legislators are grateful for your input.

COMMUNICATING WITH LEGISLATORS BY LETTER

Identify your target legislators. You can send a letter to your own representatives, to all members of a committee dealing with your issue, or to the entire legislative body.

Mention a specific issue and/or bill. Your letter will be more effective if it concentrates on a specific issue or a particular bill. When referring to a bill, cite the sponsor, bill title, and number. If possible, include the bill's status: what committee it has been referred to, when the public hearing was held.

Dear Representative Jones:

I am writing to urge your support of L.D. 2214, An Act to Ensure Safety for Workers, which was presented for public hearing before the Legislature's Labor Committee last Tuesday, February 10th.

Be brief and succinct. A one-page letter has more impact than a ten-page letter. Outline your main point in the first paragraph and try to cover only one issue per letter. Make it clear how you want the legislator to vote. For background, you could also include a newspaper clipping or fact sheet that discusses the issue in greater depth.

Make it personal. Policymakers and their staff are more likely to pay attention and remember letters that include real-life experiences. Explain why the issue is important to you, how the legislation will affect you and others in your area. Describe an experience you've had that illustrates your point. Organized campaigns do not impress legislators as much as heartfelt constituent communication.

Identify your relationship with the legislator. If you are a constituent or have another connection with the legislator, say so at the beginning. Include your name and address. This enables the legislator to respond to your letter. Your address also indicates your voting district, and gives an extra incentive for the legislator to pay attention to you.

Ensure that they receive the letter. When the legislature is in session, send your letter to the state capitol building; out of session, use the district (or home) address.

Follow up. Make a quick call to confirm receipt of the letter. You can simply say to the receptionist: "I'm calling Representative X to make sure she received my letter about L.D. 2214, the Act to Ensure Safety for Workers." Leave your name and phone number. Call or write until you get an acknowledgment of your letter.

Send a final reminder about the bill. Find out when the bill will be voted on and, just before the vote, send a postcard (or leave a phone message) about your position. As before, include the bill number and title. This will let the legislator know you are following this issue, and that the vote is still important to you.

Thank the legislator if he or she voted with your position.

Face-to-Face Visits

Schedule a meeting. Call the legislator's office and schedule a meeting enough in advance that you have time to prepare. Confirm the meeting, and invite other people working on this issue. Keep a record of who attended, what information was shared, and any actions promised.

Be flexible. Expect interruptions and changes in schedule or staff availability. If you can't meet with a legislator, try to meet with an appropriate staff member or reschedule for another time.

Staff people are extremely important and may have great influence on a legislator's views.

Be prompt. Don't be late, as it sets a bad tone for the meeting before it has even started. If you are running late, call ahead and let the legislator's office know.

Be prepared. Make the most of your visit: plan your presentation in advance and divide up roles for group members to take on, including a note taker. Plan a five-minute presentation (ten minutes at the most) and expect to spend no more than 15 minutes with the legislator. Make your important points in a clear and succinct manner. Note personal relationships and constituents.

Take advantage of opportunities. Meetings with legislators can take place anywhere—in the state house hallways, the district office, or the local grocery store. Take advantage of unexpected opportunities to speak with legislators.

Leave something behind. Develop a handout packet to leave with the legislator. It should include a short (one to two pages) summary of your group, the issue you are working on and your request for action, background information about the issue, and press clippings such as editorial support for your position.

By Telephone

Identify yourself using your name and address. If you are a constituent, say so.

Identify the issue you want to talk about; when referring to a bill use its number and title.

State both your position and how you would like the legislator to vote.

Ask for the legislator's position on the bill or issue. If supportive, ask for a commitment to vote for your position. If opposing or undecided, thank them for the information—don't argue with them on the phone. Ask what information would be helpful in helping the legislator become a proponent.
If the legislator is unavailable, *leave a detailed message* with a staff member. The staff member may be able to describe the legislator's position.

Follow up by sending a note thanking the legislator for their time. Include any information that the legislator can use to solidify their position, or which may move them to support your position.

In Testimony

When committees and subcommittees hear views from a constituent on a certain topic, it is called "testimony." Arrangements for presenting testimony vary by state: the state legislative research office or your legislator will be able to describe the procedure in your state. In most areas, you can arrange to present testimony by calling the bill's sponsor, the chair of the committee considering the bill, or your legislator. Once you've scheduled your testimony:

- Draft a five-minute speech on the bill. Begin by thanking the committee for allowing you to present your views. Make the testimony interesting, personal, and compelling.

- Include information about what the bill's effects would be, as well as a few compelling statistics about the situation the bill is designed to address.
- Print your testimony. Include your name, address, organizational affiliation, and the bill number at the top of the first page. Find out from the committee staff how many copies of your testimony to bring to the hearing.
- Attach easy-to-read background information (such as a fact sheet or newspaper article) to each copy of your testimony.
- Practice delivering your testimony so you won't be nervous. Time your delivery to ensure that you have enough time.
- Expect questions from the legislators, particularly from those opposing your viewpoint, and be prepared to address their concerns.

What to Do If the Legislator...

Strongly agrees with your position: Thank them.

Ask them to take a leadership role in the legislature, the media, and/or the community.

It is appropriate to ask for any of the following, and more: an agreement to write an article for a newsletter; signature on a petition or letter of support; public use of legislator's name; sponsorship of a bill; agreement to offer amendments to legislation; speeches at public forums; agreement to vote for or against a resolution.

Ask their advice about who else to talk to, what arguments make the best case for the bill, what media strategy will be most effective in gathering support for the bill.

Ask what information or constituency would be helpful in swaying additional legislators to your position. Then work to produce these materials or advocates.

Ask them to "lobby" undecided legislators and give them a list of these legislators. Thank them again.

Is undecided or noncommittal: Inform them of your interest in the issue or legislation.

Present the case clearly and concisely. If possible, have constituents and/or teens make the presentation.

Ask about their viewpoint to investigate whether their position results from personal or political factors, a lack of information, misinformation, or a combination. Adjust your strategy accordingly.

Ask if there are specific groups or individuals from whom they would like to hear.

Offer to provide information that will help inform them about the issue.

Follow up by providing information they requested or information addressing their reservations.

Once they have indicated a position, thank them for their support, or send a letter stating your disappointment in their position.

Keep in touch to nurture the relationship.

Is opposed to your position: Thank the legislator for the opportunity to discuss your views.

Determine how strong their opposition is and upon what it is based. If the opposition is not vehement, it may be worth trying to change the legislator's position.

If the legislator appears movable, present information that addresses his or her concerns. Make sure that the legislator hears from constituents who support your position. Strategize and present the case most likely to resonate with this particular legislator.

Stay in touch to nurture the relationship with the legislator.

If the legislator is not movable, ask them not to lobby their colleagues on the issue. With a close vote, where you cannot win unless the legislator cooperates, ask them to "walk" (be absent) when the vote occurs.

If the legislator's opposition is strong, write and express your disappointment in their position (and/or their vote). Don't waste your time and energy trying to move them.

Reprinted with permission from Advocating for Adolescent Reproductive and Sexual Health: The Advocacy Kit, *copyright © 1996 by Advocates for Youth, 1025 Vermont Avenue, NW, Suite 200, Washington, DC 20005.*

CASE STUDY

Zion United Church of Christ
Henderson, Kentucky

Rev. J. Bennett Guess

Zion United Church of Christ, a just-peace, open, and affirming congregation in Henderson, Kentucky, has been involved in a wide range of reproductive health care ministries. Established in 1871, Zion Church has a strong history of peace and justice work, and the congregation sees its support of full-options family planning, unintended pregnancy and disease prevention, women's health care, and HIV/AIDS ministry as an extension of our faith-based commitment to the people of our immediate neighborhood and city. Zion UCC has 200 members; the city of Henderson has 30,000 residents in a metro area of about 350,000.

The congregation has a strong commitment to openness and healing—two traits that have enabled us to move forward in courageous ways. The church has a strong alliance with the lesbian, gay, bisexual, and transgender community and this relationship has opened the doors for more honest discussion about sexuality among our parishioners. When the city found itself with no viable HIV/AIDS organization and a growing number of HIV/AIDS cases, the people of Zion created what is now an ecumenical, interfaith care provider. Also, the congregation is one of only a few to have initiated a parish nursing program to encourage holistic health care within the parish.

The Paff Haus, which is Zion UCC's adjacent peace and justice center, has a great track record of initiating and cultivating progressive entities in the city. So, in 1995 when leaders in the women's community began to lament the lack of a Planned Parenthood Clinic in Henderson, the Paff Haus staff/volunteers and the people of the Zion Community got involved. The relocation of the city's downtown health department, which once had been located only a few blocks from the church but was moved to a suburban neighborhood, heightened the need for reproductive health care services in the church's downtown area. Recognizing that at least one-third of the city's poor lived within a ten-block radius surrounding the church and the Paff Haus, the congregation rallied in support of the clinic idea.

An innovative arrangement between two Planned Parenthood affiliates (Planned Parenthood of Louisville and Planned Parenthood of Central and Southern Indiana), coupled with support from the Zion UCC community, the Henderson County NOW chapter, and a venture grant from the Planned Parenthood Federation of America, made the two-year project a reality. In the summer of 1997, the Henderson Health Center, operated by Planned Parenthood, was opened.

Some right-wing, antichoice, anti-birth control activity organized in opposition to Zion UCC and the opening of an on-site Planned Parenthood Clinic in Henderson. To some extent, the right-wing rhetoric was successful in framing the debate solely around the issue of abortion, even though abortions are not offered at the Henderson facility.

91

However, since the clinic has opened, the congregation has been involved in educating the general public about women's special health issues, the need for reproductive health care options, and the good services that Planned Parenthood provides.

Quality reproductive health care certainly includes the option of obtaining a safe, legal abortion, but it is certainly larger than any single issue or procedure. It involves prevention, birth control, health screenings, information, support, planning, and alternatives. We learned firsthand that the antichoice voices are also clearly opposed to birth control and comprehensive sexuality education. In an effort to stop the clinic's opening, opposition voices employed antigay rhetoric (in reference to the church's open and affirming position) and racist arguments that falsely claimed Planned Parenthood was antipeople of color. We are proud to say that the right wing's "divide and conquer" strategies failed. Support for the clinic by persons of all races, backgrounds, and religious beliefs was strong.

Incidentally, the Paff Haus at Zion UCC—where the clinic is located—also includes an office of the Villages of Kentucky, a foster care and adoption agency. In November 1997, the Religious Coalition for Reproductive Choice honored Zion UCC for being the first congregation in the country to open an on-site reproductive health care clinic—a distinction that the congregation was not even aware existed.

The people of Zion, who have long understood the intersection of justice issues, found out just how true it is. For us, the opening of a Planned Parenthood clinic and the opposition we faced became a symbol of this connection, in terms of identifying and uncovering racism, sexism, classism, and homophobia. We remain committed to the clinic's success and to further involvement in health care ministries and courageous acts for justice.

The Reverend J. Bennett Guess is pastor of the Zion United Church of Christ in Henderson, Kentucky.

Hemet, California

Rev. Sarah Gibb Millspaugh

Between 1993 and 1996, the citizens of Hemet, California, successfully organized to end the use of an abstinence-only curriculum in the public schools. Hemet, a city of 50,000 with a large population of retirees, is located in the San Jacinto Valley, approximately 80 miles southeast of Los Angeles.

In 1989, the Hemet Unified School District (HUSD) began using *Sex Respect: The Option of True Sexual Freedom* as its sexuality education curriculum. *Sex Respect* had been introduced to the district by Bonnie Park, a local teacher who was later elected to the HUSD governing board. This abstinence-only curriculum, which has been used in thousands of public and private schools since the mid-1980s, has been a source of controversy in a number of communities. In Shreveport, Louisiana, it was found to violate state law by including medical misinformation, counseling on abortion, specific religious teaching, and quizzing about personal beliefs.

In March 1993, Hemet parent Maureen Bryan filed a complaint against *Sex Respect* with the school district, seeking the removal of the curriculum. Bryan found the curriculum to be "utterly inappropriate because of its religious bias, its overt counseling against abortion, and its perpetuation of stereotypes that don't belong in a public environment" and to be in violation of the California Education Code. Park, now on the school board, countered by asserting that curriculum opponents were "on a mission to get rid of *Sex Respect* because it isn't politically correct. It doesn't promote the safe-sex agenda ... the homosexual agenda."

The HUSD governing board, a majority of whom were affiliated with the religious right, rejected Bryan's petition, voting in December 1993 to continue use of *Sex Respect* for the remainder of the 1993-94 school year. When Bryan appealed that decision in January of 1994, the board authorized an advisory committee to develop a curriculum for the 1994-95 school year, but declined to rule out the use of *Sex Respect* in future years.

While Bryan appealed to the school board, Vicki Rufsvold, a Lutheran working her way toward the ministry, began to organize local parents and people of faith to stand in opposition to the curriculum and to the characterization of its opponents as godless. Thanks to her efforts, the Interfaith Community Alliance (ICA), an organization "dedicated to the preservation of our cherished constitutional rights, especially religious freedom, and the principle of separation of church and state," was born in November 1993. In a 1994 letter to *Mother Jones*, Hemet parent Nan Creighton explained the group's mission: "In the November 1992 election, members of the religious right gained a majority on our school board. After a year of struggle and frustration at being labeled immoral, anti-God liberals for opposing the board majority, a group from several of the community's moderate churches formed the Interfaith Community Alliance. We realized the best way to ensure diversity and individual freedom was to concentrate our efforts on safe-guarding the separation between church and state."

The ICA faced a number of challenges in Hemet, a politically conservative commu-nity. While the ICA was composed of people of faith, no ordained clergy were among them. The group was asked by the Lutheran church to find an alternative meeting space after controversy in the church made hosting the group difficult. The ICA subsequently met at a Methodist church, and later at a Presbyterian church. According to ICA member (and later president) Karl Puechl, the group was perceived by many as "rabble-rousing radicals."

In September 1994, the school board rebuffed protesters by voting to formally adopt *Sex Respect* in its entirety. The ICA responded by organizing a rally "to draw pub-lic attention toward the critical issues facing public education in this community." The "Freedom Fest" attracted national press attention, and actors Christopher Reeve and Mike Farrell were among the speakers. Yet, despite this event and months of advocacy work, the ICA lost its first major fight: to elect candidates to the school board who would sup-port comprehensive sexuality education and the separation of church and state in the schools. After the November election, conservatives still held a 4-3 majority.

Meanwhile, just before the election, 11 Hemet parents filed a lawsuit against the school district over its decision to adopt *Sex Respect*. Attorneys from People for the American Way and the Planned Parenthood Federation of America filed the suit on be-half of the parents, seeking an injunction to prevent the district from using materials that promote abstinence as the only acceptable form of birth control. "Nobody wants to sue their school district," Hemet parent Maureen Bryan told *Education Week*, October 12, 1994. "But when you've tried everything, sometimes your only recourse is going to court."

Over the next two years, the ICA continued to make its presence known. At least three ICA members attended every school board meeting, whether or not sexuality edu-cation was discussed. The ICA protested the teaching of creationism in the Hemet pub-lic schools, advocated against a constitutional amendment on prayer in the schools, and worked to hold school board members accountable for inaccurate or biased statements on all issues.

Meanwhile, the lawsuit progressed. According to a spokesperson for People for the American Way, attorneys argued that the Hemet School Board violated California law by requiring the use of sexuality education materials that are "heavily promoted by right wing political groups and are replete with medical inaccuracies regarding the prevention of AIDS/HIV transmission and unintended pregnancy.... The lawsuit further alleged that the board adopted the materials against the recommendations of its own attorneys, the district's Teachers' Committee, and a Curriculum Council consisting of teachers, parents, and students."

In April of 1996, the Hemet parents and the HUSD governing board settled the law-suit. As a result, *Sex Respect* was taken out of Hemet schools and a medically accurate HIV/AIDS education curriculum took its place. Parents could now choose between two different AIDS education courses for their teenagers: an "expanded program" that would provide additional instructional materials to promote healthy behavior, and a "minimum program" that offered only the minimum HIV/AIDS education required by California law.

Later that year, the ICA again rallied around the school board elections. In this election, the group chose a more moderate strategy: to solicit and publicize the views of all candidates and encourage members to vote for the candidate of their choice, rather than to endorse specific candidates and contribute further to community schism. The strategy appeared to work, as a 4-3 majority of moderates was elected to the board. "We do not know to what extent we can claim credit, but we do know that we now have an HUSD Governing Board that can function smoothly and, we hope, effectively; one attuned to our community's educational desires and goals," an ICA newsletter proclaimed.

After several years of advocacy work and court battles, the Hemet schools still lacked a comprehensive sexuality education curriculum. (A fall 1997 proposal to adopt one failed by one vote.) Yet, in the removal of a misleading curriculum, the reinstatement of HIV/AIDS education, and the election of a more moderate school board, the Hemet citizens accomplished much. ICA board member Sue Jordan described her experience this way: "When we lost the election in 1994 things looked, felt, and seemed incredibly bleak. We had counted on winning to turn things around. When that didn't happen we could have given up, or we could have given in to the petty squabbles that frequently plague grassroots organizations. But we didn't.... For two years we did what needed to be done. We turned up the heat. We worked the media. We got the rumor mill working in our favor. We convinced the mushy middle that the time had come. And it had."

Resources for More Information

SEXUALITY EDUCATION CURRICULA

Our Whole Lives

A lifespan comprehensive sexuality education series published by the Unitarian Universalist Association and the United Church Board for Homeland Ministries. The series includes:

> *Our Whole Lives: Sexuality Education for Grades K-1*, by Barbara Sprung
>
> *Our Whole Lives: Sexuality Education for Grades 4-6*, by Elizabeth M. Casparian, PhD and Eva S. Goldfarb, PhD
>
> *Our Whole Lives: Sexuality Education for Grades 7-9*, by Pamela M. Wilson, MSW
>
> *Our Whole Lives: Sexuality Education for Grades 10-12*, by Eva S. Goldfarb, PhD and Elizabeth M. Casparian, PhD
>
> *Our Whole Lives: Sexuality Education for Young Adults, Ages 18-35*, by Michael Tino, MDiv, PhD, Sarah Gibb Millspaugh, MDiv, and Laura Anne Stuart, MPH
>
> *Our Whole Lives: Sexuality Education for Adults*, by Richard Kimball

The series also includes the *Our Whole Lives Parent Guide for Grades K-1 and 4-6* written by the Reverend Patricia Hoertdoerfer. The United Church Board for Homeland Ministries and the Unitarian Universalist Association have designed companion programs, entitled *Sexuality and Our Faith*, for each level of *Our Whole Lives*. The companion programs incorporate worship and religious values into each of the programs' sessions. To order *Our Whole Lives* or *Sexuality and Our Faith*, contact the Unitarian Universalist Association Bookstore at 25 Beacon Street, Boston, Massachusetts 02108-2800, 800/215-9076, bookstore@uua.org or http://www.uua.org/bookstore.

Created in God's Image: A Human Sexuality Resource for Ministry

A program for adults that focuses on the integration of sexuality into the ministry and mission of the church. It is based on a needs assessment survey which showed that 83 percent of UCC members want the church to be a resource to them as they make sexuality-related decisions and address sexuality-related concerns. For more information contact: Created in God's Image Coordinator, United Church of Christ, 700 Prospect Avenue,

Cleveland, OH 44115-1100, 216/736-3718.
http://www.ucc.org/justice/sexuality-education/created-on-gods-image/adult.html

Affirming Persons, Saving Lives

A faith-based HIV/AIDS education curriculum for kindergarten through adults developed by the United Church Board for Homeland Ministries. For more information contact: United Church of Christ, 700 Prospect Avenue, Cleveland, OH 44115-1100, 216/736-3718.

Many major denominations and religious groups also publish sexuality education curricula, which vary in their comprehensiveness and religious content. Contact your denomination's local or national offices for details. You may also consult *A Time to Speak: Faith Communities and Sexuality Education*, by Debra W. Haffner, which contains an annotated listing of sexuality education curricula designed by faith communities. The book is available from SIECUS, listed below under "Sexuality Education and Sexual Health."

Organizations such as Advocates for Youth also publish curricula; see their contact information below under "Sexuality Education and Sexual Health." Many Planned Parenthood affiliates maintain libraries of sexuality education curricula—contact your local Planned Parenthood for more information.

SEXUALITY EDUCATION AND SEXUAL HEALTH: INFORMATION AND ADVOCACY

Advocates for Youth
2000 M Street NW
Suite 750
Washington, DC 20036
202/419-3420
http://www.advocatesforyouth.org

Produces resources for sexuality educators including fact sheets, curricula, programs, and advocacy materials. Programs include: HIV education and prevention, teen pregnancy prevention, peer education, media education, parent/child communication, support for lesbian, gay, bisexual, and transgender youth, and a support center for school-based and school-linked health care. Numerous publications, including a sexuality education advocacy kit.

Comprehensive Health Education Foundation (CHEF)
159 S. Jackson St., Ste 510
Seattle, WA 98014
800/323-2433
email: info@chef.org
http://www.chef.org

Supports schools, youth organizations, and faith communities with curricula, training, resources, and conferences.

National Campaign to Prevent Teen and Unplanned Pregnancy
1776 Massachusetts Ave., NW, Ste. 200
Washington, DC 20036
202/478-8500
http://www.thenationalcampaign.org

Publishes resources, including some specifically for faith communities. Supports a Religion and Public Values Task Force.

The Network for Family Life Education
Rutgers, The State University
100 Joyce Kilmer Avenue
Piscataway, NJ 08854-8045
Website under development

A coalition of public, private, and nonprofit agencies joined in support of family life education—including comprehensive instruction about human sexuality—in school and community settings. Resources include two newsletters: "Family Life Matters" and "Sex, Etc."

Planned Parenthood Federation of America
434 West 33rd Street
New York, NY 10001
212/541-7800
http://www.plannedparenthood.org

The Planned Parenthood Federation of America provides comprehensive reproductive and complementary health care services, advocates for public policies that guarantee these rights and ensure access to such services; and provides educational programs that enhance understanding of individual and societal implications of human sexuality. Planned Parenthood has affiliate organizations and clinics throughout the United States that offer resources to sexuality educators. Planned Parenthood Federation of America supports two pro-choice networks of people of faith: the Pro-Choice Religious Network and the Clergy for Choice Network.

Sex Information and Education Council of Canada (SIECCAN)
850 Coxwell Avenue
Toronto, Ontario, CANADA M4C5R1
416/466-5304
email: sieccun@web.ca
http;//sieccan.org

Publishes The Canadian Journal of Human Sexuality, *a peer-reviewed, academic journal and the SIECCAN Newsletter, which contains articles and resource reviews for sexuality educators. Their resource, "Common Questions About Sexual Health Education," is designed to assist Canadian sexuality education advocates. (Note: SIECCAN is not affiliated with SIECUS, below.)*

Sexuality Information and Education Council of the United States (SIECUS)
90 John St., Suite 402
New York, NY 10038
212/819-9770
http://www.siecus.org

Develops, collects, and disseminates information, promotes comprehensive sexuality education, and advocates for the right of individuals to make responsible sexual choices. Provides program consultation and assistance to communities. Publications include Guidelines for Comprehensive Sexuality Education, Community Action Kit, *the bimonthly* SIECUS Report, *and the* SIECUS Advocates Report. *Resources and projects related to religion and sexuality include annotated bibliographies of books and curricula,* A Time to Speak: Faith Communities and Sexuality Education *by Debra W. Haffner, and the Religion and Sexuality Initiative, designed to assist religious institutions in implementing sexuality education in their congregations. Also supports the SIECUS Public Policy office in Washington, DC. (Note: SIECUS is not affiliated with SIECCAN, above.)*

Guttmacher Institute
125 Maiden Lane, 7th floor
New York, NY 10038
212/248-1111 (toll free: 800/355-0244)
http://www.guttmacher.org

Conducts reproductive health research, policy analysis, and public education. Publishes Family Planning Perspectives *newsletter plus fact sheets and resources on family planning, adolescent health, and maternal and child health.*

Centers for Disease Control and Prevention (CDC)
National Prevention Information Network (NPIN)
PO Box 6003
Rockville, MD 20849-6003
800/458-5231
email: info@cdcnpin.org
http://www.cdcnpin.org

A national reference, referral, and distribution service for information on HIV/AIDS and STDs run by the United States Centers for Disease Control.

ETR Associates
4 Carbonero Way
Scotts Valley, CA 95066
831/438-4060
http://www.etr.org

Provides leadership, educational resources, training, and research in health promotion with an emphasis on sexuality and health education. Produces numerous health education resources for clinic, community, and educational settings.

Health Canada
AL 0900C2
Ottawa, Ontario, Canada K1A 0K9
613/957-2991 (toll free: 866/225-0709)
email: info@hc-sc.gc.ca
http://www.hc-sc.gc.ca

Health Canada is the federal department responsible for helping the people of Canada maintain and improve their health. The Health Canada home page includes extensive information on many aspects of health, including sexuality education, HIV/AIDS, and STDs. The department's Health Promotion Home Page (http://www.hc-sc.gc.ca/hppb/hpo/index.html) includes information about HIV/AIDS and Comprehensive School Health.

National School Board Association (NSBA)
HIV and AIDS Education Project
1680 Duke Street
Alexandria, VA 22314
703/838-672
email: info@nsba.org
http://www.nsba.org

Helps policymakers and educators make informed decisions about HIV and AIDS policy and education issues. Has established a continuously updated resource database of HIV and AIDS policy.

RELIGIOUS ORGANIZATIONS CONCERNED WITH SEXUALITY ISSUES, DOMESTIC VIOLENCE, AND REPRODUCTIVE CHOICE

The Balm in Gilead
701 East Franklin St., Ste.1000
Richmond, VA 23219
804/644-2256 (BALM)
http://www.balmingilead.org

Works through Black churches to stop the spread of HIV in the African-American community and to support those infected with and affected by HIV and AIDS.

Black Church and Domestic Violence Institute
3645 Marketplace Blvd., Ste.130-375
East Point, GA 30344
707/909-0715
email: bcdvorg@aol.com
http://www.bcdvi.org/fr_this farbyfaith.cfm

A project of the Center for the Prevention of Sexual and Domestic Violence (see below). Develops programs and resources for use in African-American congregations.

Catholics for a Free Choice
1436 U Street, NW, Suite 301
Washington, DC 20009
202/986-6093
email: cfc@catholicsforchoice.org
http://www.cath4choice.org

Conducts policy analysis, education, and advocacy on issues of gender equity and reproductive health.

National Council of Churches (NCCC)
Committee on Family Ministries and Human Sexuality
475 Riverside Drive, Room 800
New York, NY 10115
212/870-2228
http://ncccusa.org

A committee composed of representatives from religious denominations and member organizations. Assists participating denominations and organizations in addressing human sexuality throughout the life cycle.

The Park Ridge Center for the Study of Health, Faith, and Ethics
205 West Touhy Ave., Ste. 203
Park Ridge, IL 60068-4202
837/384-3507
http://www.parkridgecenter.org

The Project on Religion, Sexuality, and Public Policy helps decision makers understand issues related to sexuality and policy and works with religious leaders and communities.

Religious Coalition for Reproductive Choice
1413 K Street NW, 14th floor
Washington, DC 20005
202/628-7700
http://www.rcrc.org

Works to ensure reproductive choice through the moral power of religious communities. All of its programs seek to give voice to the reproductive issues of under-served populations, including people of color and those living in poverty. The RCRC Black Churches Initiative (http://www.rcrc.org/bci) focuses on promoting reproductive health, supporting sexuality education, and reducing teenage pregnancy in African-American communities.

Religious Consultation on Population, Reproductive Health, and Ethics
2823 North Summit
Milwaukee, WI 53211
414/961-0139
http://www.igc.apc.org/consultation

International multifaith network of progressive feminist religious scholars and leaders. Addresses population, consumption, ecology, and reproductive health issues.

Religious Institute: Faithful Voices on Sexuality and Religion
www. religiousinstitute.org

Provides resources for congregations, communities and families. UU minister Debra Haffner is co-founder and director.

Search Institute
615 First Ave. NE
Minneapolis, MN 55413
800/888-7828
http://www.search-institute.org

An independent, nonprofit organization dedicated to research and practices benefiting children and youth. Research and resources available for religious communities.

Vanderbilt University Divinity School
Carpenter Program in Religion, Gender, and Sexuality
411 21st Avenue South
Nashville, TN 37240
615/936-8453
http://www.vanderbilt.edu/divinity/carpenter

The Carpenter Program's mission is to foster conversation on the subject areas of religion, gender, and sexuality within and across religious affiliations, ideological bases, and cultural contexts.

BISEXUAL, GAY, LESBIAN, AND TRANSGENDER ISSUES

The Gay, Lesbian, and Straight Education Network (GLSEN)
90 Broad Street, 2nd floor
New York, NY 10004
212/727-0135
emai: glsen@glsen.org
http://www.glsen.org

Brings together teachers, parents, students, and concerned citizens on a national and local level to work together to end homophobia in our schools. Focuses on in-school programming, advocacy, and community organizing.

Interweave Continental
156 Massapoag Ave.
Sharon, MA 02067
email: webmaster@interweaveuu.org
http://interweaveuu.org

A membership organization affiliated with the Unitarian Universalist Association. Dedicated to the spiritual, political, and social well-being of Unitarian Universalists who are confronting oppression as lesbians, gay men, bisexuals, and transgender persons, and their heterosexual allies.

Open Hands: Resources for Ministries Affirming the Diversity of Human Sexuality
3801 North Keeler Avenue
Chicago, IL 60641
773/736-5526
email: openhands@RMNetwork.org
http://www.chrisglaser.com/openhands.html

Open Hands is a quarterly magazine of the ecumenical welcoming church movement. Published cooperatively with the Reconciling Congregation (Methodist), More Light (Presbyterian), Open and Affirming (Disciples of Christ), Open and Affirming (United Church of Christ), Reconciled in Christ (Lutheran), and Welcoming and Affirming (Baptist) church programs.

Parents, Families, and Friends of Lesbians and Gays (PFLAG)
National Office
1828 L Street, NW
Suite 660
Washington, DC 20036
202/467-8180
email: info@pflag.org
http://www.pflag.org

Supports local chapters throughout the United States, Canada, and world. Publishes resources for families and allies of gay, lesbian, bisexual, and transgender people as well as resources for those who are coming out.

Office of Bisexual, Gay, Lesbian, and Transgender Concerns
Unitarian Universalist Association
25 Beacon Street
Boston, MA 02108
617/742-2100, x470
email: lgbt@uua.org
http://www.uua.org/obgltc

Resources include educational, ceremonial, and program materials; consultation; workshop leadership; advocacy; information and referral; and conflict resolution. Supports the Welcoming Congregation, a program for Unitarian Universalist congregations that confronts heterosexism and homophobia.

Office for Lesbian, Gay, Bisexual, and Transgender Concerns
United Church of Christ
700 Prospect Avenue
Cleveland, OH 44115
216/736-2100
http://www.ucc.org

Provides consultation to congregations, pastors, and laypeople on lesbian, gay, bisexual, and transgender issues. Offers resources for study, including bibliographies, videos, and a compendium of United Church of Christ policy on lesbian, gay, bisexual, and transgender concerns. The office staff offer workshops and presentations for a variety of audiences.

United Church of Christ Lesbian, Gay, Bisexual, and Transgender Ministries
Rev. Michael Schuenemeyer
Executive for Health and Wholeness Advocacy
700 Prospect Ave.
Cleveland, OH 44115
216/736-3217
email: schuenem@ucc.org
www.ucc.org/lgbt

An officially recognized interest group of the United Church of Christ. Organizes National Gatherings each summer. Administers the "Open and Affirming" Program (ONA), which encourages local congregations to declare themselves open and affirming to people of all sexual orientations. Supports regional, conference, and chapter activities. Advocates for change in church and society.

MONITORING AND COUNTERING THE RELIGIOUS RIGHT

American Civil Liberties Union
125 Broad Street, 18th Floor
New York, NY 10004-2400
212/549-2500
http://www.aclu.org

Litigates, legislates, and educates on issues that affect individual freedom in the United States, including sexuality education, religious liberty, and lesbian and gay rights. National and state chapters.

Americans United for Separation of Church and State
1301 K. Street, NW, Ste. 850, East Tower
Washington, DC 20005
202/466-3234
email: americansunited@au.org
http://www.au.org

Engages in education, litigation, advocacy, and media work to protect religious freedom. State and local chapters.

The Interfaith Alliance
1212 New York Ave., NW, Ste. 1250
Washington, DC 20005
202/238-3300
http://www.interfaithalliance.org

A nonpartisan organization committed to the positive role of religion as a healing and constructive force in public life. Challenges groups such as the Christian Coalition that use religion to promote an extreme political agenda. Local and state chapters throughout the United States.

People for the American Way (PFAW)
2000 M Street, Suite 400
Washington, DC 20036
202/467-4999
http://www.pfaw.org

The PFAW Freedom to Learn Project monitors school censorship activity, including censorship of sexuality education programs. PFAW's Freedom to Learn Action Kit includes specific information to help citizens combat censorship, as well as advice for activists responding to highly organized challenges.

Political Research Associates
1310 Broadway, Ste. 201
Somerville, MA 02144
617/666-5300
email: pra@publiceye.org
http://www.publiceye.org

A nonprofit research group that monitors political extremists and maintains a library of far-right wing literature.

OTHER ADVOCACY RESOURCES

Communications Leadership Institute
The SPIN Project
3555 18th Street
San Francisco, CA 94110
415/829-7719
http://www.spinproject.org

Helps develop the capacity of grassroots groups to shape public opinion and garner positive media attention through media education and training. The SPIN Project's Web site contains easily accessible resources for working with the media.

Family Health Productions, Inc.
PO Box 1639
Gloucester, MA 01930
978/282-9970
e-mail: info@abouthealth.com
http://www.abouthealth.com

A nonprofit production company (formerly Media Works) that produces and distributes television programs, videos, companion guides, and books about public health and sexuality education advocacy. Videos include: Raising Healthy Kids: Families Talk About Sexual Health, Risky Times: How to Be AIDS Smart and Be Healthy, In Our Own Words: Teens and AIDS, *and* What Works: Sexuality Education.

UNITARIAN UNIVERSALIST AND UNITED CHURCH OF CHRIST OFFICES

United Church Board for Homeland Ministries
700 Prospect Avenue
Cleveland, OH 44115
216/736-3718
http://www.ucc.org

A United Church of Christ board for ministry and mission, serving congregations throughout the United States, including Puerto Rico. Provides consultation and support to congregations regarding the Our Whole Lives, Affirming Persons, Saving Lives, *and* Created in God's Image *sexuality education programs.*

Justice and Witness Ministries: Washington Office
United Church of Christ
100 Maryland Avenue, NE
Washington, DC 20002
202/543-1517
www.ucc.org/justice/washington-dc

Empowers efforts to shape public policy decisions based on the values of the church as expressed by the United Church of Christ General Synod. Provides and publishes information and literature on social issues, cooperates with instrumentalities of the United Church of Christ and with other appropriate bodies in creating social change, supports leadership development initiatives, and formulates and promotes a program of social education and action for the United Church of Christ.

Unitarian Universalist Association of Congregations
25 Beacon Street
Boston, MA 02108
617/742-2100
http://www.uua.org

An association of Unitarian Universalist congregations throughout the United States and Canada. The Unitarian Universalist Association's Department of Religious Education provides consultation and support to congregations regarding the Our Whole Lives *sexuality education program.*

Canadian Unitarian Council
100-344 Dupont Street
Toronto, Ontario M5R 1V9
416/489-4121 (toll free: 888/568-5723)
email: info@cuc.ca
http://www.cuc.ca

The national association of Unitarian and Universalist congregations in Canada. Provides support for religious exploration, spiritual growth, and social responsibility.

United Church of Christ
Resolutions and Pronouncements
on Sexuality Issues

The following resolutions and pronouncements were passed by the General Synod of the United Church of Christ in the years indicated. The General Synod, composed of delegates from congregations throughout the United States, convenes biannually to determine church policy and conduct the business of the United Church of Christ.

Freedom of Choice Concerning Abortion: A Proposal for Action—1971

> Calls for action and education leading to the repeal of legal prohibitions of physician-performed abortions.

General Synod reaffirms the right of women to freedom of choice with regard to pregnancy—1973, 1977, 1979

Civil Liberties Without Discrimination Related to Affectional or Sexual Preference—1975

> Proclaims the Christian conviction that all persons are entitled to full civil liberties and equal protection under the law.

Human Sexuality and the Needs of Gay and Bisexual Persons—1975

> Expresses support for gay, lesbian, and bisexual persons in professional church leadership. Commissions a study concerning human sexuality and the theological basis for a Christian ethic concerning sexuality.

Recommendations in Regard to the Human Sexuality Study—1977

> Adopts "Human Sexuality: A Preliminary Report," in addition to 18 specific points. Urges support for sexuality education in schools, adult education programs, social welfare agencies, medical services, and communications media.

Deploring the Violation of Civil Rights of Gay and Bisexual Persons—1977

> Deplores the use of Scripture to generate hatred and the violation of civil rights of gay and bisexual persons.

Resolution on Freedom of Choice—1981

> Opposes the passage of constitutional amendments and legislation that would revoke the freedom to choose abortion.

Institutionalized Homophobia Within the United Church of Christ—1983

> Calls for the elimination of institutionalized homophobia in all its forms.

In Response to the Concerns of Same-Gender Oriented Persons and Their Families Within the United Church of Christ—1983

> Reaffirms the United Church of Christ's commitment to family ministry to all, regardless of family composition.

Acquired Immune Deficiency Syndrome (AIDS)—1983

> Calls for research, education, and legislation to address the AIDS epidemic.

Recommending Inclusiveness on Association Church and Ministry Committees Within the United Church of Christ—1983

> Calls for continuing education to increase understanding of gay and lesbian persons and their commitment to the Christian faith. Recommends openness to the nomination and election of lesbian and gay laypersons and clergy to church and ministry committees.

Report of the Task Force for the Study of Human Sexuality—1983

> Receives the report of the Task Force for the Study of Human Sexuality. Urges the support of educational programs to teach about human sexuality and to end sexual violence.

Calling on United Church of Christ Congregations to Declare Themselves Open and Affirming—1985

> Encourages congregations to adopt a policy of nondiscrimination against lesbian, gay, and bisexual people, and to adopt a Covenant of Openness and Affirmation of persons of lesbian, gay, and bisexual orientation.

Resolution on Pornography—1987

> Articulates the General Synod's abhorrence of pornography Urges ministry to victimizers and victims of violence, pornography, and sexual abuse.

The Right to Privacy—1987

> Affirms the right to privacy for all adults in their private, consensual, and sexual relationships, free from government intrusion. Urges work for legislation that guarantees the civil liberties of all without regard to sexual orientation.

Sexuality & Abortion, A Faithful Response—1987

> Reaffirms the right of women to reproductive choice. Urges the United Church of Christ to provide educational resource to help reduce unplanned pregnancies and to encourage responsible sexual behavior.

Health and Wholeness in the Midst of a Pandemic—1987

> Calls for HIV/AIDS education for all; government funding of HIV/AIDS research, service, education, treatment, and prevention; and sexuality education programs, beginning early in elementary school.

Sexual Harassment in the Church—No Longer Nameless—1989

> Calls upon the United Church of Christ, its member congregations, and other UCC institutions to undertake educational programs on the issue of Christian ethics dealing with sexual harassment and abuse within pastoral, professional, and personal relationships in the church.

General Synod reaffirms the United Church of Christ's support for a woman's right to choose a safe, legal abortion—1989

Deploring Violence Against Lesbian and Gay People—1989

> Calls for education and legislation to end violence against lesbian and gay people, as well as other oppressed groups.

Responding to AIDS: An Audit of AIDS Discrimination in the United Church of Christ—1989

> Directs the Executive Council of the United Church of Christ to conduct a church-wide audit to evaluate the nature and degree of AIDS discrimination within the church. Calls for the alleviation of discrimination discovered as a result of the audit.

Responding to AIDS: Endorsement and Enactment of the "Ten Principles for the Workplace"—1989

> Endorses a list of ten principles designed to guarantee the workplace rights of people with HIV/AIDS.

Affirming Gay, Lesbian, and Bisexual Persons and Their Ministries—1991

> Affirms, celebrates, and embraces the gifts of ministry of lesbian, gay, and bisexual persons. Calls upon congregations, associations, and conferences to adopt an "Open and Affirming" policy and to extend welcome and support to openly lesbian, gay, and bisexual ministerial students and candidates.

Virginia Privacy Laws—1991

> Calls upon the Virginia Legislature to repeal the Virginia sodomy laws and other laws directed at persons specifically because of their sexual orientation.

Calling on the Church for Greater Leadership to End Discrimination Against Gay People and Lesbians—1993

> Calls for legislation, education, and leadership to end the legal sanctioning of discrimination against gays and lesbians.

Faithfulness in Committed Relationships—1997

> Reaffirms that the standard for sexual and relational behavior for members of the United Church of Christ is fidelity and integrity in marriage or other covenanted relationships, in singleness, and in all relationships of life.

Female Genital Mutilation—1997

> Calls for US immigration officials to consider female genital mutilation a type of extreme harm and a violation of human rights qualifying one for protection under the Refugee Act.

The full text of each listed resolution can be obtained from the United Church of Christ's Office of the Secretary, 216/736-2100. The United Church of Christ General Synod has also passed resolutions related to Women's Rights—contact the UCC Coordinating Center for Women at 216/736-2150 to obtain a listing.

Unitarian Universalist Resolutions
on Sexuality Issues

The following resolutions were passed by the Unitarian Universalist Association General Assembly in the years indicated. The General Assembly, composed of delegates from congregations throughout the United States and Canada, convenes annually to conduct the business of the Unitarian Universalist Association.

(Resolutions marked with an "IW" are resolutions of "Immediate Witness." These resolutions are voted upon at the same Unitarian Universalist Association General Assembly at which they are proposed. Because they do not go through the two-year congregational review process afforded all General Resolutions, they do not represent the policy of the Unitarian Universalist Association but rather the concerted voice of the individual delegates at the time of voting.)

Reform of Abortion Statutes—1963

Supported the legalization of abortion in certain cases.

Abortion—1968

Called for the abolition of all existing abortion laws except for the law that prohibits the performance of abortions by unlicensed physicians.

Support for Ministers Involved in Counseling Services for Problem Pregnancies—1969

Expresses support and encouragement for ministers who counsel women with problem pregnancies.

Discrimination Against Homosexuals and Bisexuals—1970

Urges an end to discrimination in employment on the basis of sexual orientation.

Equal Rights and Opportunities for Women—1970

Calls for education, legislation, and action to end discrimination against women.

Abortion—1973

Supports the US Supreme Court ruling on abortion.

Creation of an Office on Gay Affairs—1973, Office of Gay Concerns—1974, Office of Gay Concerns—1975 (The title of this office evolved to its present designation, Office of Bisexual, Gay, Lesbian, and Transgender Concerns.)

> Three resolutions establishing an office at Unitarian Universalist Association head-quarters to work to achieve the goals of the 1970 resolution "Discrimination Against Homosexuals and Bisexuals" and to act as a resource to the denomination.

For the Right to Abortion—1975

> Reaffirms the right of women of all ages to abortion services regardless of marital or economic status.

Older Women—1976

> Expresses support for the challenges faced by older women due to ageism and sexism.

Equal Rights Amendment—1977, ERA Emergency Action—1977, UUA Meetings and Non-ERA Ratified States—1978, Equal Rights Amendment—1983

> Resolutions supporting local and national advocacy for the ratification of an amend-ment to the US Constitution guaranteeing women and men equal rights.

Gay Human Rights—1977

> Calls for work to stop biased persecution and intolerance of gay people.

Women and Religion—1977

> Calls upon Unitarian Universalists to examine sexist assumptions inherent in their religious literature and institutions.

Abortion: Right to Choose—1978

> Reaffirms the Unitarian Universalist Association's support of abortion rights.

Battered Women—1979

> Urges Unitarian Universalist individuals and congregations to be advocates for bat-tered women and to examine religious myths that perpetuate violence against women.

Ministerial Employment Opportunities—1980

> Urges UUA to lend full assistance to the settlement of openly gay, lesbian, and bi-sexual religious leaders.

A Religious Statement on Abortion: A Call to Commitment—1980

> Endorses the Religious Coalition for Abortion Rights' (now known as the Religious Coalition for Reproductive Choice) religious statement on abortion and urges that educational programs be "pressed forward" to reduce unplanned pregnancy by fos-tering responsibility in sexual conduct.

Implementation of Women and Religion Resolution—1980

> Calls for the use of nonsexist language and the development of materials to help congregations eradicate longstanding sexist assumptions.

United Nations Convention for the Elimination of Discrimination Against Women—1981

> Expresses support for this United Nations convention.

Gay and Lesbian Services of Union—1984

> Affirms Unitarian Universalist ministers' leadership of services of union for same-sex couples and urges the development of resources to support ministers who perform these ceremonies.

Materials on Sexual Abuse—1985

> Urges the Religious Education Department of the Unitarian Universalist Association to make sexual abuse prevention resources available for children and youth.

Opposing AIDS Discrimination—1986

> Opposes discrimination based on AIDS, the fear of AIDS, or the presence of HIV.

Ending Gender-Based Wage Discrimination—1987

> Encourages action to eliminate gender-based wage discrimination within the Unitarian Universalist Association and within society at large.

Supporting Legal Equity for Gays and Lesbians—1987

> Calls upon the Unitarian Universalist Association to support the recision of sodomy laws and to support the adoption of laws prohibiting discrimination based on sexual orientation.

Right to Choose—1987

> Reaffirms the Unitarian Universalist Association's support for abortion rights. Calls on Unitarian Universalists to work productively with those who oppose abortion rights to promote family planning and responsible sexuality education.

Proposals of the Common Vision Planning Committee—1989

> Establishes the Welcoming Congregation program, which certifies congregations that have gone through a process to examine homophobia and heterosexism and welcome gay, lesbian, bisexual, and/or transgender people.

The Travel Rights of HIV-Infected People—1989 (IW)

> Condemns the United States government's imprisonment and deportation of HIV-infected people attempting to enter the United States.

Youth in Crisis—1990

Called for advocacy on behalf of youth, including support for school-based clinics and other providers of family planning services.

Rights of Privacy and Free Speech—1991 (IW)

Urges the enactment of legislation that will ensure that birth control information and counseling about problem pregnancy options, including abortion, be made available to women without parental notification or consent.

Opposing Legalization of Discrimination Against Gays, Lesbians, and Bisexuals—1992 (IW)

Condemned antigay ballot initiatives introduced in Colorado and Oregon.

Response to the June 29, 1992 United States Supreme Court Decision Upholding Pennsylvania's Constraints on Women's Reproductive Freedom—1992 (IW)

Condemns the Court's upholding of constraints on abortion rights. Demands full support of law and justice agencies in controlling violence against providers of reproductive health services.

Acceptance of Openly Lesbian, Gay, and Bisexual Persons in the United States Military—1993 (IW)

Urged support for lifting the ban on openly lesbian, gay, and bisexual individuals serving in the US armed forces.

Federal Legislation for Choice—1993

Urges the passage of federal legislation to guarantee the right of individual choice in reproductive matters, regardless of age, class, race, or situation.

Violence Against Women—1993

Calls upon Unitarian Universalists to take a number of steps, including advocating for the introduction of school curricula that promote gender equality and respect.

Sexuality Education in the Public Schools—1994 (IW)

Urges Unitarian Universalist congregations to advocate for comprehensive sexuality education programs taught by trained teachers in the public schools and to make congregation-based sexuality education programs available to youth in the congregation and community at large.

Support the Employment Nondiscrimination Act of 1994—1994 (IW)

Supports the passage of federal legislation guaranteeing nondiscrimination against gay, lesbian, and bisexual people.

In Support of the Right to Marry for Same-Sex Couples—1996 (IW)

> Urges support of the legal recognition of same-sex marriage.

Challenging the Radical Right—1996

> Urges Unitarian Universalists to challenge the radical right and to proclaim and promote Unitarian Universalist principles by participating in public institutions such as schools, libraries, political parties, and governmental bodies.

Support for Nondiscriminatory Corporate and Other Business Policies—1997 (IW)

> Encourages the support of businesses that have policies of nondiscrimination on the basis of sexual orientation or gender identity.

> *The full text of these resolutions can be obtained from the Unitarian Universalist Association's Department for Faith in Action: 617/742-2100, x454.*

Sexuality Education Curriculum Components

Our Whole Lives: Sexuality Education for Grades K-1
by Barbara Sprung. Eight one-hour sessions.

Sexuality and Our Faith: A Companion to Our Whole Lives Grades K-1
Unitarian Universalist: by Rev. Patricia Hoertdoerfer and Rev. Makanah Elizabeth Morriss
United Church of Christ: by Rev. John M. Barrett and Faith Adams Johnson

Our Whole Lives: Sexuality Education for Grades 4-6
by Elizabeth M. Casparian, Ph.D, and Eva S. Goldfarb, Ph.D. Eight one-hour sessions.

> To be used with: *It's Perfectly Normal: Changing Bodies, Growing Up, Sex and Sexual Health*,
> by Robie Harris, illustrated by Michael Emberley, Candlewick Press, 1994.

Sexuality and Our Faith: A Companion to Our Whole Lives Grades 4-6
Unitarian Universalist: by Rev. Patricia Hoertdoerfer and Rev. Makanah Elizabeth Morriss
United Church of Christ: by Rev. John M. Barrett and Faith Adams Johnson

The Parent Guide to Our Whole Lives Grades K-1 and Grades 4-6
by Rev. Patricia Hoertdoerfer

Our Whole Lives: Sexuality Education for Grades 7-9
by Pamela M. Wilson, MSW. Twenty-seven ninety-minute sessions.

Sexuality and Our Faith: A Companion to Our Whole Lives Grades 7-9
Unitarian Universalist: by Rev. Makanah Elizabeth Morriss and Rev. Jory Agate
United Church of Christ: by Rev. Lizanne Bassham and Rev. Gordon J. Svoboda II

> Slides to accompany religious supplements to *Our Whole Lives Grades 7-9*. Black and white
> drawings. Script and discussion guide included.

Our Whole Lives: Sexuality Education for Grades 10-12
by Eva S. Goldfarb, Ph.D. and Elizabeth M. Casparian, Ph.D. Twelve two-hour sessions.

Sexuality and Our Faith: A Companion to Our Whole Lives Grades 10-12
Unitarian Universalist: by Rev. Makanah Elizabeth Morriss, Rev. Jory Agate, and Rev. Sarah Gibb
Millspaugh
United Church of Christ: by Rev. Lizanne Bassham and Rev. Gordon J. Svoboda II

> Video to accompany religious supplements to *Our Whole Lives Grades 10-12*. Script by Eva S.
> Goldfarb, Ph.D. and Elizabeth M. Casparian, Ph.D. Produced by Mark Schoen, Ph.D.

Our Whole Lives: Sexuality Education for Young Adults, Ages 18-35
by Rev. Michael J. Tino, Rev. Sarah Gibb Millspaugh, and Laura Anne Stuart, MPH. Fourteen
two-hour sessions

Our Whole Lives: Sexuality Education for Adults
by Richard S. Kimball. Fourteen two-hour sessions.

Sexuality and Our Faith: A Companion to Our Whole Lives for Adults
Unitarian Universalist: by Judith A. Frediani

The Advocacy Manual for Sexuality Education, Health and Justice: Resources for Communities of Faith
Rev. Sarah Gibb MIllspaugh, editor